Scarlet Thunder

Sigmund Brouwer

orca sports

Orca Book Publishers

Library and Archives Canada Cataloguing in Publication

Brouwer, Sigmund, 1959-
Scarlet Thunder / written by Sigmund Brouwer.

(Orca sports)
ISBN 978-1-55143-911-2

I. Title. II. Series.
PS8553.R68467S3 2008   jC813'.54   C2007-907178-3

Summary: Trenton suspects that someone is sabotaging the documentary
about stock-car racing that he is helping his uncle film.

First published in the United States, 2008
Library of Congress Control Number: 2007941812

Orca Book Publishers gratefully acknowledges the support for its publishing
programs provided by the following agencies: the Government of Canada
through the Book Publishing Industry Development Program and the Canada
Council for the Arts, and the Province of British Columbia through the BC Arts
Council and the Book Publishing Tax Credit.

Cover design by Teresa Bubela
Cover photography by Masterfile
Author photo by Bill Bilsley

Orca Book Publishers   Orca Book Publishers
PO Box 5626, Stn. B   PO Box 468
Victoria, BC Canada   Custer, WA USA
V8R 6S4   98240-0468

www.orcabook.com
Printed and bound in Canada.

11 10 09 08 • 4 3 2 1

chapter one

I really didn't want to climb the steps to knock on the door of the trailer.

I stood at the bottom, holding a cup of coffee in my hand. Well, not coffee. Latte.

Lah-tay. Only uncivilized beasts said it wrong.

Lah-tay. As ordered, it was made from freshly ground Brazilian coffee beans. With skim milk, steamed but not too hot. With fresh whipped cream on top. Sprinkled with cinnamon and chocolate shavings.

Not served in a paper cup. Not served in a mug. But delivered in a cup made of thin china. On a saucer. With a real silver spoon on the side.

This latte was for Hunter Gunn, the famous movie star. He was waiting, probably impatiently, inside the trailer. And to make sure everyone on the set understood that the big trailer was for his use only, he had insisted that his name be painted on its door. Painted. He was only going to be here for three days. But then, it had cost ten thousand dollars to rent the trailer he had demanded. So what was a couple hundred extra to put his name on it?

I sighed and climbed the steps. Even though my uncle was in charge here, he made me start at the bottom. That meant I was a gopher—as in "go for" whatever you're told to fetch. That meant my job was to run around and do errands. Like this one.

I knocked.

No answer.

I knocked louder.

Still no answer.

I knocked even louder.

"What's with all the pounding out there?" a voice hollered from within. It was a voice that millions of people had heard, usually when Hunter Gunn was saving the world from asteroids or terrorists armed with nuclear bombs.

"Well, I tried knocking softly but—"

"Don't back-talk me! I don't care who your uncle is. I can buy him and a dozen like him if I want to."

"Yes, sir," I said. My uncle, Mike Hiser, was directing this commercial shoot. I felt stupid talking to a painted name on a door that was only a few inches from my face.

"Why are you bothering me?" the voice demanded.

"I have your coffee, sir," I said. I grinned, because I knew exactly what I'd hear next.

"Lah-tay!" the voice almost screamed. "Lah-tay! Only uncivilized beasts drink coffee."

A person had to take what satisfaction he could from someone who could buy his uncle and a dozen like him.

"Yes, sir," I said, biting my grin. "Latte. I have it here."

"What took you so long?" the voice growled.

Hunter Gunn had only called for his drink five minutes earlier. And it had taken three minutes to make. Two minutes for delivery wasn't that bad.

"Sorry, sir," I said. I waited for him to open the door.

He didn't.

I stood on the steps and looked over the fence into the San Diego Zoo. It was a high fence, screened by heavy bushes and palm trees. A big area of the parking lot had been taped off for our stuff. And to keep us safe from traffic.

I waited some more.

I was glad today was the last part of this shoot. We just had to finish a scene with Hunter Gunn and an elephant. That's why we had set up at the zoo instead of a studio lot in Hollywood. Even with the cost of Hunter Gunn's rented trailer, it was cheaper to come to the elephant than it was to bring the elephant to us.

I kept waiting. The morning sun felt good. San Diego in the summer didn't seem as hot and dry and smoggy as Los Angeles.

I waited longer, thinking about where my uncle and I would go next. Tomorrow, we were headed east to begin a stock car racing documentary. A television sports channel had already agreed to air the special. Filming it was the most fun I'd have this summer. It was—

The door suddenly opened. I stood face-to-face with Hunter Gunn, with his silk shirt and designer jeans, his handsome face, his thick blond hair, his bright blue eyes and his fifteen-million-dollar-a-movie smile.

But he wasn't smiling.

And I wasn't actually face-to-face with him. I was taller than Hunter. Most people were. But he always insisted the camera shoot him at an upward angle to make him look tall.

Without a word, he snatched the china cup and saucer from my hand.

He took a sip.

"This is cold," he said. He poured the liquid on the steps, and some of it splashed my shoes. "Get me a hot cup."

"Yes, sir," I said. I didn't point out that it had gotten cold while I had waited for him to come to the door. After the first hour with Hunter Gunn, I had come to expect this sort of treatment.

I started to walk away.

"Don't forget to mix the cinnamon and chocolate shavings in equal portions," he said. "Last time you used too much cinnamon."

"Yes, sir," I responded.

I didn't think the day was going to get much better. Not if Hunter Gunn thought he could treat a two-ton elephant the way he treated people.

chapter two

"Junior Louis is a real sweetheart," Walter Merideth, the animal trainer, said. He was a short, wide, older man with a big grin and a ragged haircut. "Hardly anything excites him."

Good thing, I thought.

Junior Louis looked anything but junior. I mean, everyone knows elephants are big, but I didn't realize how big until I got up close to one. Junior Louis put me and the trainer in shadow. Junior Louis seemed like a building covered with thick hide. He stood patiently, flicking his tail back and forth at flies. Every once in a while he flapped his ears, but other than that, he was a statue, rooted to the pavement.

"What about mice?" I asked. "Does Junior Louis get excited about mice? You know, like in the old *Bugs Bunny* cartoon?"

I love *Bugs Bunny*. There's this one cartoon where a big elephant goes crazy trying to get away from a mouse.

The trainer laughed.

"I've seen that cartoon too," he said. "It's funny, you're the second person to ask me that today."

He patted Junior Louis on the leg. "Yes, there is some truth in it. Seems silly that something this big would get nervous about something so tiny. But the fact is that some mice are small enough to get up inside an elephant's trunk."

I wrinkled my nose. The trainer caught me doing it and laughed again.

"Think about it," he said. "In the wild, elephants feed themselves by pulling grass with their trunks and stuffing it into their mouths. In captivity, they scoop up hay the same way. And where else would mice hide but in grass or hay? Elephants tend to grab a big bunch all at once. So anytime an elephant eats, there's a chance that it might scoop up a mouse. It's not likely that a mouse would ever scoot up inside an elephant's trunk, but imagine the thought of eating a salad and finding a worm or a cockroach, or having a bug crawl up your nose or into your ear while you slept..."

I wrinkled my face more and gave a little shudder.

"Exactly," the trainer said. "Elephants like those thoughts about as well as you do." He shrugged. "But it's not like we're going to see a lot of mice out here in a parking lot."

Before I could agree with him, I heard a big, wet, plopping sound. On pavement.

I looked behind Junior Louis. Then I groaned. Elephants do everything in a big way. And as gopher, I got to do all the dirty work around the set.

And Junior Louis had just supplied me with a lot of dirty work.

"Excuse me," I said to the trainer. "I think I'll need a shovel and a wheelbarrow for this job."

When I finished about fifteen minutes later, Uncle Mike was just about ready to begin filming. This commercial was supposed to show the strength of a certain brand of underarm deodorant.

The fact that Hunter Gunn had agreed to act in it told me two things. First, his career was on the way down if he was willing to do a commercial like this one. And second, the deodorant company was paying big money for the commercial. I knew that from reading the weekly trade papers. Hunter Gunn's career wasn't that far gone yet.

I stayed with the trainer as he led Junior Louis into position. There were three cameramen, each behind a big camera on wheels, each wearing a headset to hear my uncle's directions better. A fourth cameraman had a position in the crane. My uncle wanted the scene recorded from four angles. Later, he'd cut the various angles into one shot.

There were also about a hundred extras, some makeup people and a dozen people from the zoo. We were all doing what people usually do during a shoot.

Nothing.

Sometimes it takes a couple of hours to film a ten-second scene. This was one of those times. In this part of the commercial, the elephant goes crazy during a hometown parade. Hunter Gunn, our hero, jumps on it and rides it like a horse, saving the people lined up to watch the parade. The point of the commercial is supposed to be that the deodorant keeps people—Hunter Gunn, in particular—from sweating, no matter how scary the situation.

I stayed near Junior Louis, thinking that no amount of deodorant would keep me from sweating if he went crazy, even if I was in an armored tank. I was also thinking that Junior Louis could use some deodorant himself...and maybe an oversized diaper.

Uncle Mike stepped into the center of the setup shot.

11

"Listen up, folks," he said. All conversation stopped. He was known as a very fair person, but one with little patience. Which, for a director, is a good thing. Sometimes it costs tens of thousands of dollars a day to get a scene on film; every minute counts.

"Thank you," he said. He was medium height and square shouldered. His nose was big, but his large forehead and solid chin balanced it. He had curly hair, mostly dark, and wore blue jeans, a gray T-shirt and a *Mickey Mouse* cap. Because they're identical twins, my uncle looks just like my father. And I look a lot like them. Except at seventeen I don't have the wrinkles around my eyes or gray hair at my temples.

"Folks," Uncle Mike said, "as you know, in this scene Mr. Gunn will ride the runaway elephant. But please, please, please, do not move. Not yet. We need to get a few close-up shots of Mr. Gunn on the elephant first. Later, when the elephant is off the set, we'll get you to run around and scream with panic. Understand? Absolutely no screaming or running now. We don't want to spook Junior Louis."

Even if they didn't understand how this would all come together, I did. To television viewers, it would look like Hunter Gunn had leaped on the elephant's shoulders as it ran through a crowd of people who were getting stomped. Then it would look like Hunter Gunn was holding the strap around the elephant's head and battling it to a standstill.

In real life, though, it would work a lot differently. Uncle Mike would take a bunch of shots of the actor on the elephant. Hunter Gunn's face would show the emotions of a man riding a wild elephant to a standstill. After that, away from all the people, a stunt man dressed like Hunter Gunn would get on the elephant and try to hang on as it galloped a short distance. These shots would get cut into the commercial, among other shots of people screaming and running away. Edited and mixed together, it would look very real.

Here, in the parking lot, it would look very boring.

And it should have been boring.

Of course, as the elephant's trainer said later, who could have guessed what was in the cooler?

chapter three

From the beginning of this three-day shoot, Hunter Gunn had insisted on having a cooler nearby, filled with freshly blended vegetable juices. He was terribly worried about the sun damaging his skin. Whenever he had to stand around outside, he dabbed some juice on his face, then covered it with a steamed towel.

I thought it was dumb. But I was just a gopher. And if he thought mashing vegetables on his skin would keep him from looking older, I was in no position to disagree.

Every twenty minutes or so, as we waited, it was my job to bring him fresh steamed towels. The towels were simple to get ready. I just soaked them in water and stuck them in a microwave. Then I brought them out on a platter, which made me feel like a silly waiter.

Hunter Gunn had barked out the now-familiar order for steamed towels as he stood beside Junior Louis. Both Gunn and the elephant were waiting for some final camera and lighting adjustments.

I ran for the towels, heated them and ran back.

Hunter Gunn was still standing beside Junior Louis. Every few minutes, the elephant tried to rest his trunk on the actor's shoulder. Hunter Gunn shooed the trunk away.

"Find me two stools," Gunn said to me.

Then he glared at the trainer and demanded, "Get this stupid beast to leave me alone."

I didn't hear the trainer's answer because I was already jumping at Hunter's command.

I looked around at the clutter. Cables lay on the ground in all directions. People stood and sat anywhere they could perch. Parked vehicles lined the edges of our shoot.

I spotted two stools, grabbed them and ran back to Hunter Gunn.

"Finally," he said with an exaggerated sigh. "Now put my cooler on one and my platter of towels on the other. If you barbarians are going to insist I wait out here instead of in the quiet of my trailer, the least you can do is make me comfortable. I will not squat on the ground to apply my natural sunscreen."

I wanted to tell him that sunscreen in a bottle was way cheaper and way more convenient. But I wasn't some wacky health guru charging him thousands of dollars.

I put the cooler on one stool and the platter on the other.

I stepped back.

Hunter Gunn opened the cooler's lid.

And mice swarmed out of the cooler and up his arms.

Mice. Lots of tiny mice, frantic to find someplace safe to hide.

17

Mice scampered up Hunter's arms before he even knew what was happening.

Junior Louis, though, with his trunk resting close to Hunter's shoulder, knew exactly what was happening.

Junior Louis bellowed a high-pitched scream of terror that sent people running in all directions.

A mouse jumped onto Hunter Gunn's head.

Junior Louis swatted at the mouse with his trunk.

The actor screamed and fell to his knees.

The elephant rose onto his back feet.

The trainer ran to grab the chain around Junior Louis's neck.

People screamed.

Mice ran every which way.

Junior Louis bellowed. He landed on his front feet and flailed his trunk at the darting mice.

With the trainer hanging on to his chain, Junior Louis took off. He half ran, plowing into a camera, dragging his trainer.

Hunter lay on the ground, crying.

Junior Louis stopped when he reached the fence at the edge of the parking lot.

And just like that, it was over.

There was no sign of any mice.

The shoot had been ruined.

Hunter Gunn lay curled up in a ball, whimpering.

I took a double take, amazed. He was bald. Completely bald.

I saw something near him on the pavement that looked like a dead cat. A blond dead cat. I went over and picked it up. A wig.

I was, after all, the set gopher.

I walked over to the cowering, sniffling actor.

"Here you are, sir," I said matter-of-factly, handing him his wig. This moment was worth whatever delay it would cost Uncle Mike. I tried to hide my smile as I politely asked, "Should I bring you a box of tissue?"

chapter four

"Not Long Pond!" Uncle Mike screamed into his cell phone. "Loudon! Loudon, in New Hampshire. Not Long Pond, in Pennsylvania!"

He wasn't screaming in anger. Instead, he was yelling to be heard above the roar of engines. Uncle Mike and I stood in the parking lot outside the racetrack in New Hampshire. Two weeks had passed since Junior Louis exposed Hunter Gunn's bald head to the world. Now it was the day before the qualifying runs here, and racers on the track were in the middle of trials.

A hot wind swept over us, bringing grit off the parking lot like ashes from a fire. The sky was totally blue, with no hint of clouds to bring relief from the heat. The pavement seemed to burn through the soles of my shoes. It was not a great place to stand and listen while Uncle Mike tried to work through the confusion with his secretary on the phone.

"No, definitely not," Uncle Mike yelled. "Why would I have asked you to ship the stuff to Long Pond when I knew I was coming to Loudon? Long Pond is later in the schedule."

He listened quietly, frowning with frustration.

"Look," Uncle Mike said. "I know they sound similar. Maybe you misheard me when I asked you to fill out the shipping forms. It doesn't matter whose fault it is. I need that equipment yesterday. Find the truck, stop it and get the stuff on an airplane."

A long pause. I guessed his secretary was calling the shipping company on another line.

"Tomorrow?" he yelled. "Tomorrow? You've got to get the stuff here today! I don't care what it costs us. If it's not here today, we're in trouble."

He snapped the cell phone shut.

"Not good, Trent," he said to me. He pointed at the racetrack behind us. "Somehow our gear is headed toward the wrong city. I mean, if it was already there, it wouldn't be so bad. We could have it reshipped. The stuff could be here by this afternoon, and we'd only lose half a day."

At ten thousand dollars a day for crew and expenses, half a day was bad enough.

"Where is it?" I asked.

"Somewhere between California and Pennsylvania," he said. "On a truck. Somehow it got shipped by ground instead of overnight by air. And to the wrong place. I don't get it. My secretary doesn't usually make mistakes like this."

He shook his head. "As if I need this to worry about. On top of everything else."

Everything else included the mice in the cooler. No one could figure out how they'd gotten there. That little episode had delayed the commercial three days. And Hunter Gunn had demanded extra salary to continue. That, with the cost of delays, had come out of Uncle Mike's budget. He'd told me that his production company had actually lost money on the deal. The commercial was supposed to have made him fifty thousand dollars.

"If we only miss a day," I said, "it can't be that bad. At least not compared to—"

"Don't remind me about Junior Louis," he said. "And yes, it is bad. The mess with Junior Louis made us miss last week's race. So every day we miss now is crucial. Extremely crucial. I absolutely have to deliver this documentary on time.

"I haven't told any of the crew about the urgency to make this deadline. I didn't think it was something to worry about," he continued. "I mean, when I signed the deal, I figured there was no way to miss."

"Miss?"

"You know my company is simply a production company. I'm doing this under contract to Lone Coyote Studios, who in turn will make money by selling the documentary to the sports network."

I knew all that. My big ambition was to be a director. I wanted that more than anything else in the world. I wanted it so bad that I thought about nothing else. So whatever I read or listened to or watched was all related to the film industry.

Uncle Mike continued. "My contract with Lone Coyote Studios promises delivery of the finished one-hour documentary by August fifteenth. Because the airtime is worth a lot of advertising dollars to the racing team's sponsor, if we deliver on time my company will get a huge bonus: one million dollars."

"The bonus is great," I said. "But the deadline..."

I'd been hanging out with Uncle Mike's small film company for five summers. Long enough to know something about the business. After we finished filming, we would need several weeks in post-production to get the piece ready. In other words, we were cutting it close already.

"Exactly," he said. "It's already July, and we're running out of time. And there's a reverse bonus built into the contract. My company gets fined two hundred thousand dollars for every day the project's late."

I whistled as I did my math. "On time is worth a million. Five days late costs a million."

"Scary," he agreed. "I agreed to the terms, because I need the bonus to get the next project I have in mind going. It's one that could make my career as a director. I just never dreamed we would be late, so I figured it would be worth the risk. But with all the problems we've been having..."

Yeah, I thought. This was the first summer I had seen such big things go wrong. The mice in the cooler had caused delays and huge unexpected costs. And now, with the gear lost somewhere on a highway between us and California, this project wasn't looking good.

My face must have shown my worry.

"There is one piece of good news," Uncle Mike said, trying to cheer me up. "At least for you."

"Me?" I asked.

"Yup. You. I want you on a camera this shoot."

"What?!?" I nearly yelled in my excitement.

"Think of it as a promotion for all the summers you've spent as my gopher—and as thanks for the hours of research you've done to help me understand racing. I want you to use a handheld, shooting whatever you think might look good. I'm not making any promises about how much of your footage we'll use, but consider yourself your own director. You get to choose what to shoot and what angles to shoot from. Play it like a music video. I'll take care of the main cameras, but I want you to look for the little touches that can add depth to the documentary."

"Cool," I said. "Really cool."

At that moment, I stupidly believed this was going to be my best summer yet.

chapter five

You can watch high-speed stock-car racing all you want on television, but you'll never really know what it's like unless you've been there. Don't get me wrong, I find it exciting enough to watch on television. But it doesn't come close to the electricity of being there in person.

It was early on qualifying day, so the stands were only three-quarters full. Still, that was about a hundred thousand people. Yeah. A hundred thousand. Which is just a big number until you look up from the pits. Then you see a wall of brightly colored shirts about a half mile long and dozens and dozens of rows high. The roar of the crowd, a high-powered hum of energy, somehow rises above the pounding thunder of the full-throttled cars that sometimes reach two hundred miles an hour.

You never really understand what two hundred miles an hour is either, not from television. The camera follows the car, and you see the car get bigger and smaller as it comes and goes. But when you're standing there beside the track, you have to snap your head from side to side to follow a car as it flashes by. Two hundred miles an hour is a blur of screaming color. At that speed, the car goes a mile in under twenty seconds. Some airplanes don't go that fast.

But being at the track is about more than what you see. Or hear. There's also the vibration from those huge howling engines...the rumbling of the ground... the smell of high-octane gasoline...and the excitement of the crew in the pit area, something edgy that spills over and gives you the same fear and thrill.

I knew, because that's where I stood. Right in the middle of the pit crew.

Their attention was on a bright red Chevy covered with logos and decals. It had come off the track after a practice run. It stopped in front of us. And the driver got out of the car.

With so many people gathered near the car, no one really seemed to notice Uncle Mike or me. So we just watched.

The pit crew wore red coveralls with a big, white, oval patch on the back. Inside the white oval I recognized the logo of a famous chewing gum. I knew from the research that I had done for Uncle Mike that the gum company was the major sponsor of the Scarlet Thunder racing team.

A tall guy with a lean face and a crew cut seemed to be in charge. I knew his name because of the photographs I'd seen of the team. He was the crew chief: George Lot.

He spoke to the driver.

"How's the car feel, Sandy?"

"It's too light through the turns," the driver said through the open visor of the crash helmet.

If I hadn't known ahead of time why we were here to film, I would have been surprised by the driver's high soft voice. And I would have been even more surprised at the long blond hair that tumbled free when the driver removed the crash helmet.

Sandy Peterson.

She was one of the sport's hottest rookies. Some people thought she was great for racing. Others didn't like her. She had quite a reputation. She was never afraid to speak her mind, and she wouldn't back down when fighting for what was right. She was a great subject for a television special.

Because I had trained myself to see things as if they were filmed and already edited, I wished we had our cameras. I wanted to catch Sandy as she stood among the pit crew. There was a smear of dirt on her forehead, making her light blue eyes seem even bluer.

Sweaty strands of hair stuck to her face. She ran her fingers through her hair as she continued to speak.

"In fact," she said to George, "there's a wobble there that I don't like. I'm pretty sure it's the rear spoiler. I think I'd like the angle set a little higher."

During the past five summers with Uncle Mike, I had heard him say again and again that a good director should know as much as possible about a subject before coming to a set. Because of that, I had spent hours and hours and hours reading all I could about stock-car racing. And because of that, I knew the basics about the back spoiler.

As a car travels at high speeds, it cuts through the air. The air flows over the car and catches on the rear spoiler. That pushes the back end of the car down. The higher the spoiler's angle—the more straight up it is—the more air it catches. The good thing about the downward force is that it pushes the tires toward the ground and makes the car less likely to skid. The bad thing is the trade-off. While more air pushing the car down makes it more stable, it also makes the car slower.

"Set the angle on the rear spoiler higher?" another man said. He moved closer to George and Sandy, almost pushing his way between them. "You could bleed away half a second per lap."

This man was a shorter, slimmer version of George Lot, but with long hair parted in the middle. I searched my memory and came up with a name for the face. Lance Lot. George's younger brother.

Lance turned his focus toward George. "That spoiler's set at sixty-seven degrees. That gives us the max speed for this track. And we need max speed to win. We can't do that with a driver who's afraid to drive."

Everyone seemed to freeze.

"Lance, this is not the time or place," George began. "If you have concerns, bring them to me in private."

"No," Sandy said. "I'd rather deal with this in the open. If your brother wants to drive, he should prove himself in a race car.

If not, he can keep his mouth shut. He's not the one who will kiss a concrete wall if the back end slips going into a corner."

I wished double hard we had the cameras going. Funny thing is, after a day or two, no one notices them. Sure, the first day, people watch what they say and how they look because they're really aware of the cameras. But if the cameras are always around, it doesn't take long for them to become part of the background. And if we had them here, this footage would be great. Just like bad news gets higher ratings, arguments are more interesting to watch than interviews.

Sandy pointed at the car behind her. "I'll bet whatever you want that the spoiler is not set at sixty-seven degrees. You may think it is, but it's not driving that way. I can feel it on the corners."

Lance spit on the ground. "I set it myself. I know I'm right. I—"

He stopped. Another pit crew member was shaking his head and pointing at the spoiler.

"Looks like someone bent this corner," the man said. "It's a bit flat."

Sandy smiled at Lance. She pushed her helmet hard into his stomach. It pushed a woof of breath out of his lungs.

"Fix it, please," she told Lance. "And find out who had a chance to mess with the spoiler and why. We don't have much more practice time before my qualifying run."

She left him holding her helmet and walked toward Uncle Mike.

"Hello," she said, smiling and extending her hand in greeting. "I'm Sandy Peterson. And you must be the famous Mike Hiser, here to give us our hour of television fame."

"It's an honor to meet you," Uncle Mike said, shaking her hand.

"So," she said, "I've got about fifteen minutes before I go back on the track. Let's sit down so you can tell me what you want to do and how you're going to do it."

chapter six

The infield of the racing track was filled with dozens and dozens of motor homes and trailers. Many racing people find it easier and cheaper to travel in a trailer as they follow the circuit from track to track.

The three of us found lawn chairs in the shade of a motor home, away from the pit crew. The shade helped but didn't give much relief from the hot wind.

Sandy looked at me as if noticing me for the first time.

"Who are you?" she asked me. "And what are you doing here?"

"This is—" Uncle Mike began.

"I didn't ask you," she said to him. "Let him answer for himself."

Uncle Mike snapped his mouth shut. I'd never heard anyone talk to him this way before.

"I'm Trenton Hiser," I said. "I do all kinds of odd jobs to help things run smoothly. But my real job is to learn as much as I can about directing."

We had to speak louder than normal to be heard above the engines revving loudly in various places along the pit road.

"Hiser," she said with a question in her voice. She jerked her thumb at Uncle Mike. "He your dad?"

I shook my head. "My uncle. My parents and sister are in Los Angeles."

I hardly thought of them when I was away. If being away from home was the price I had to pay to reach my dreams, I had decided it was worth it.

"You look too young to be out of school, let alone to think about becoming a director."

"It's summer and school is out," I said. Her amused grin showed me she was teasing. So I gave her a small grin myself. "And you look too young to drive a stock car at this level. Besides, only men should be race-car drivers."

"Trent—" Uncle Mike began.

Sandy laughed. "I deserved that. Besides, I wanted to see if he could stand up for himself. Sometimes people who get hired because they're family don't have brains or a backbone. This one does." She flashed me another grin. "We'll get along just fine."

"I'm starting to see that I can believe some of those press clippings I collected," Uncle Mike said, smiling. "What was my favorite headline?"

Tapping his teeth, he sorted through his memory. "Yes. I remember: 'Pit Bull Woman Hangs on for Victory.'"

She laughed again. "That one was better than 'Ladybug Stomps Back.'"

She shook her head. "You know, in some ways, it's great to be a woman driver. In other ways, it can drive you nuts."

Uncle Mike leaned forward. The way he did as a director when he sensed he was about to learn something that would help him frame his subject. I knew why. We had discussed this ahead of time. The thing that would make this documentary interesting was the "woman driver" angle.

"It's great," she said, "for the very reason that you're going to be hanging on every word I'm about to say. You and the rest of the world treat me differently because I'm a woman. That translates into big media exposure. Big media exposure means big sponsorship. When it costs millions a year to run a team, sponsors are important."

She looked Uncle Mike directly in the eyes. "Let's face it, if I were just another male driver, you wouldn't be here, right?"

I felt guilty, as if she had read our minds.

"Let's not forget that you have won a few races," Uncle Mike said.

"The fact that you ducked my question proves my point," she answered. "And that's what's bad about being a woman driver. People can't look past my being a woman and see me simply as a driver."

She pointed beyond us at the track. "Out there, it takes guts to survive. And, at times, almost a mean streak. Think about it. When a driver bumps your car at two hundred miles an hour to make room for himself on the track, you know it's not a tea party. Especially when a second or so between first and second place might be worth enough money to buy a house. But what happens when I bump back and send someone into the wall? He's the victim, and I'm Pit Bull Woman."

Again, I wished the cameras were here. I knew exactly what I'd do if this were my film. I'd cut back and forth between her words and some bang-bang race scenes, and there would be some real juice to it.

She looked at her watch. "Anyway," she said to Uncle Mike. "We don't have much time. Practice days are the only time I have to really learn the track; they'll have me back in the car any second. So tell me what you plan to do."

"The usual," Uncle Mike said. "Cameras everywhere. We'll get a hundred hours' worth of film and sort it out in production."

"Sounds boring," she said. "How'd you get this big creative reputation?"

"Ouch," he said. "A shot like that hurts."

"Well," she said, "there's a lot riding on this for me. The danger of giving you permission to film is that you guys might become a real distraction, and that might hurt the racing team. But on the other hand, I couldn't afford to pass up a one-hour shot at prime-time television. So make it worthwhile."

"I do have one thing in mind," Uncle Mike said, "to make this different from other documentaries."

"Good," she said.

"I want to put lightweight cameras in the car. Views out the front window and back so we can film what's happening around your car. I'd like to have you miked too.

I want you to tell us about the race as it happens: What's going through your mind. What you're trying to do as you do it. I want the viewers to feel like they're on the track right beside you."

Sandy thought about it for a second.

"You're asking a lot," she said. "Most of the time I can't afford to be distracted. It's just too dangerous. But there are times during the stretches when I might be able to talk...Okay, you can mike me, but I won't make promises about how much attention I can give you. When I need to be in contact with my pit crew or concentrate on the track, you won't hear me spelling out my race thoughts."

"No problem," Uncle Mike said. "Safety has to come first. If you'll also let us record your conversations with the crew, there should be parts we can use in the documentary."

He grinned. "Like you yelling at the pit crew. Or the pit crew yelling at you."

She didn't grin back. "You remember our contract says I get to approve the final cut?

Nothing gets on television unless it has my say-so."

"I remember," Uncle Mike said. He tried again to get a smile from her. "You think I want Pit Bull Woman mad at me?"

She didn't laugh at his little joke. "This is my career we're talking about. For you, it may be just another piece of work to add to your credits. But this is extremely important to me. It has to be just right. If not, I might lose my sponsorship. That could mean millions of dollars."

She stood. "And that's what we're up against. I've had a long streak without a win. If you do a good job, and if I manage some good finishes while you're filming, I can keep driving. It's that simple."

"Trust me," Uncle Mike said. "This is more than just another piece of work."

Yeah, I thought, it is more than just another piece of work. If we get it done on time, Uncle Mike gets a million dollars. If we don't, it could cost him a million— or more.

As for me, if we finished on time, my work might get aired on prime-time television. My name might show up on film credits for the first time. I couldn't think of anything I wanted more than that.

chapter seven

The next day, I was down at the track as Sandy Peterson got ready to take her bright red Chevy for a qualifying run.

I was early. And alone. Uncle Mike—after turning purple and nearly popping from anger—was now trying to track down equipment to rent. Our missing stuff had not arrived yet.

The worst part was that it looked like we would miss the chance to film Sandy's qualifying run, which wouldn't help our schedule.

Racing teams at this level have about thirty races a year, traveling the country from as far north as Michigan, all the way south to Florida, from Arizona to New Hampshire. It makes for a regular weekly schedule. Teams arrive at the racetrack on a Tuesday or Wednesday. The pit crews use the early part of the week to tweak the cars. The drivers use the time to get to know the track and try out the changes that the pit crews make.

Thursday and Friday are qualifying days. Only forty teams will make the cut and be allowed to race. The drivers who post lap times in the top forty then drive in Sunday's race. But qualifying means more than that. The fastest qualifiers get post positions near the front. That is important because it's a lot harder to win a race when you have to bang your way through traffic at 180 miles per hour just to find space near the front.

Saturday gave the pit crews a chance to tweak their cars some more, make repairs, even replace entire engines if necessary.

Sunday, of course, is race day. Monday's another travel day, and the cycle starts all over the next week.

We needed footage of a couple of different qualifying runs. I knew that by missing the chance to film Sandy Peterson today, we would have to wait a full week before we'd have another opportunity.

If I were filming Uncle Mike's growing desperation, I would work with a close-up shot of sand trickling out of someone's fist, like time slipping away.

Because that's what it felt like.

"You're with the film crew?"

This question was shouted into my ear above the howl of a car shooting past me. I turned.

The guy asking the question was about my height. But he looked a lot older. Blond, he had a lawyer's neat haircut. He wore dark dress pants and a white polo shirt, neatly ironed. His face was tanned, with crinkles around his eyes and at the corners of his wide smile. I'm seventeen and everyone over thirty looks ancient to me, so I could only guess his age as somewhere between thirty-five and dead.

"Yeah," I shouted back.

"Tim Becker," he said. He stuck his hand out. I shook it. The breeze running across the track pulled at my hair. But his hair stayed neatly in place, like he'd made a helmet with two cans of hairspray.

"I do public relations for Sandy Peterson," he said.

"Hi," I said. "I'm Trenton Hiser."

Only Uncle Mike called me Trent. I had decided that when I got famous, I would always insist that the world call me Trenton.

He nodded. "Thought so. Where's your uncle? I hear you guys are on a tight schedule, and Sandy's the next car on the track."

"My uncle does things his way," I answered. This guy's unspoken criticism of Uncle Mike bugged me. I didn't feel like adding that Uncle Mike's way at this moment included scrambling to rent equipment.

"Good, good," Tim said, keeping his smile wide. "I like to hear he's in control."

He didn't say anything for a few seconds. In that time, the car on the track flashed the length of about five football fields.

The car slowed and entered the pit road. It became quieter around us but not totally quiet. It seemed like there was always the sound of revving engines. But with no car screaming around the track, the sound of other engines dropped to background noise.

Tim pointed at a large electronic clock and whistled admiration.

"Look at that lap time—29.568 seconds. Close to the track record. Sandy's got her hands full if she wants to start near the front."

I knew this track was 1.058 miles long. I quickly did the math. The average time was 120 miles per hour. Average, including corners. I bet he'd gone up to two hundred on the stretches. This was the kind of drama that made for a good show. Again, I wished we were filming.

"Tell me a bit about what it takes to have a good run," I said. The more background I knew, the better.

"Sure," Tim said. "That's part of my job."

He pointed at the track. "See that ribbon of rubber?"

My eyes followed his finger. I saw a long thin line on the track, rising in places and dipping in others.

"Drivers call that the fast groove," Tim continued. "The cars lay down that rubber as they follow the best line around the track. They need to enter some turns high and come out low. With other turns, the opposite is true. It all depends on how the turn is banked. The secret is to find the line."

He moved his arm to show me some skid marks leading to the concrete wall that banked the track. "Of course, there are some lines you don't want to follow. That driver might have been on the right line, but at the wrong speed. You see the result."

I nodded.

"The right speed is everything," Tim said. "You've got to push it to the absolute max because pole positions are determined by the hundredths or thousandths of a second. A half second can cost you up to twenty-five pole positions. On the other hand, if you hit the turn too fast, you slide out of the groove. You might not crash, but it will put you out of rhythm for the next corner and cost you time."

The loudspeaker announced that Sandy Peterson was about to enter the track.

"You watch," Tim said as we both looked to the pit road for her bright red car. "She'll stand on the throttle and try to build some heat into her tires. This isn't a race, so she doesn't need to worry about wearing them out. She just wants them hot and sticky as soon as possible."

He was right. She roared onto the track. Thousands and thousands of people in the stands stood. Their yelling and screaming matched the roar of the Chevy.

"I'm a little worried about her." With the noise level up, Tim had to shout again. "She's got the car as loose as possible."

"Loose?"

"She wants maximum speed. She had the pit crew set the weight and tires and spoiler to hold the road as lightly as possible. She doesn't want anything holding her back. But that makes the car tougher to handle."

I was listening to Tim, but my eyes were following the red Chevy. As Sandy came out of the third turn, the car's back end started to slide. I expected her to steer into the skid to straighten her line.

But the slide got worse. The back end spun around and took her backward into the concrete wall.

Bang!

The car bounced off the wall and spun around so fast I couldn't count how many times it turned.

One tire came off the rear and seemed to bounce lazily across the track.

It was headed right toward us.

I didn't move because it didn't seem like a big deal. It didn't look like it was coming very fast. Then, before I knew it, the tire nearly hit us. It flew past us onto the infield and slammed into a motor home behind us.

Bang! It rocked the motor home, then settled to rest below the dent it had made.

"Um, wow," I said. I really wished I'd had the handheld camera. "That would have been awesome for the documentary."

"Wow?" Tim said. "That tire could have killed us! I feel like I've been shot at and missed. Sandy just blew a qualifying run. And all you can say is 'That would have been awesome for the documentary'? You must have ice in your veins."

"Thanks," I said. Directors aren't supposed to care about their subjects. They are just supposed to observe.

Out on the track, I saw Sandy pulling herself from the damaged car.

I was glad to see that she was okay. It would have been terrible if she had gotten hurt. Uncle Mike couldn't afford to lose more time.

chapter eight

Let me tell you what's gone wrong now," Uncle Mike said. He sat in a chair across the hotel room from me.

It was eight o'clock. Between us sat a tray full of dirty dinner dishes left from our room-service meal. Who needed a mother to cook, I always said, when all you had to do was pick up the telephone and call downstairs.

"I hope it's not a lot," I said. I really wanted to see my name on the screen.

"Since Sandy didn't qualify, we'll have to wait an entire week to get any footage of her on the track."

He leaned back in his chair and sighed. He rubbed his face with both hands. He sighed again.

"We can at least do interviews with some of the crew during the week, right?" I asked. "I mean, at least we'll be getting some work done while we wait."

"I suppose," Uncle Mike agreed. One of the great things about being his nephew was that I could be in on a lot of his brainstorming sessions. And Uncle Mike never minded listening to my ideas. "But part of what's going to make this documentary so great is tying in all the interviews to actual races. At best, all we're going to get is some background material. And meanwhile, the clock will be ticking on my deadline."

More face rubbing. "Not only that, but it looks like there are some problems with the footage we did in San Diego."

"The deodorant commercial?"

"That one," he groaned. I could tell he was thinking about the disaster with the mice. "You know how we spent all that extra time on retakes?"

I nodded.

"Somehow," he said, "a lot of that footage was out of focus. I might have to fly back to Los Angeles this week and spend a few days doing some emergency work to pull it together."

"Out of focus? Which camera?"

He shook his head. "Brian's. I just don't get it. He's normally my best cameraman. It seems like everything is going wrong lately."

"We'll still be able to finish the racing documentary on time, even if you have to go back to San Diego, won't we?" I asked.

"Only if nothing else goes wrong," he answered. "Let me tell you, if I didn't have a little backup insurance, there's no way I could sleep at night."

"Backup insurance?"

Uncle Mike grinned. "Yup. We could have a dozen disasters, and in the end, my one good break can make up for it."

He got up, poured himself a glass of water and drank it slowly. Almost like he was keeping me in suspense on purpose. But then, a good director always has a good sense of drama.

"You see," he began, "about a year ago, I read this book I really liked. It was a true-life story about a woman who ran a railroad company in the 1800s. Thing was, she knew she couldn't do business as a woman, so she disguised herself as a man and stayed in disguise her whole life. It wasn't until she died that anyone found out the truth. Now this book had been out at least ten years, and was so forgotten that I was able to buy a two-year option for only ten thousand dollars."

Ten thousand dollars was a lot of money to me. But compared to the millions sometimes spent in Hollywood, it was nothing.

And Uncle Mike didn't have to explain to me what an option was. It simply gave him the right to make the book into a movie. Nothing else. But to make the movie, he would first have to line up millions of dollars of production money. Next he'd have to line up the actors and actresses. Only then would he have to pay for the movie rights to the book, which might be a half million dollars. But if he couldn't line up money or actors, he'd be out only the original option money. And the whole time he owned the option, no one else could make the book into a movie.

"Are you curious who wrote the book?" Uncle Mike asked, grinning above his glass of water.

"Of course," I said.

"Some unknown," he said. "Which was another reason I got the option for peanuts. At least she was unknown at the time. Her name is Viola Moses."

"Viola Moses!" I said. "She's...She's..." This was so amazing, I couldn't even get the words out.

"She's the Oscar-winning screenwriter who came out of nowhere this year. Having the option to her book is like winning the lottery."

"No kidding," I said. Uncle Mike now had something that everyone in Hollywood would beg for.

"I've been making some calls over the last month," he said. "It looks like it's going to be easy to line up big money for the movie. And some big stars. This option can take me from award-winning documentaries to a major blockbuster."

"And after one blockbuster," I said, "you'll be able to pick the best movies to direct..."

He kept grinning. "And now you see why I took a chance on the deadline for this racing documentary. The million I make on the bonus will allow me to own a good chunk of the movie myself, which means even more money in the long run."

What a dream come true. Could there be anything better than fame and fortune in Hollywood?

Uncle Mike continued. "And I can't lose. Globewide Studios offered me two million for the option, right after the Oscars. That, plus they would let me direct. I told them no, because I wanted it all for myself. But if

I don't make this deadline, at the very worst, I go back to them and accept their offer."

"Sounds good," I said. "Very good. You don't have a thing to worry about."

"That's right," he said. "Nothing at all."

Wrong.

chapter nine

Finally, almost a week later, we were able to actually shoot some race footage. Our cameras and other equipment caught up with us in Talladega, Alabama, a city that looked just like all the others to me. I had learned from Uncle Mike that what really mattered was the set location. As for the different cities, they were just a hotel room repeated again and again and again.

Sandy had qualified for the race, which was great for our documentary. And today's filming location was in the Scarlet Thunder pit space, just off pit road, just off the racetrack.

There wasn't much room. Not when about forty other teams each needed a pit along the road.

Of course we gave the Scarlet Thunder pit crew all the space it needed. We fitted our cameras wherever there was space around the crew and the tires and the tanks of gasoline and the toolboxes.

Although I had a handheld camera and permission to roam wherever I wanted, I had decided to stay close to Uncle Mike. I had an idea that it would be cool to film the crew as it filmed the action. Maybe some of that footage would fit into the documentary.

I watched closely. Uncle Mike was filming Tim Becker, the public relations man. Tim was hooked up to a mike because the noise of the track was so loud. That was the only way we could get any vocals from him.

At the same time, cameraman Brian Nelson zoomed in tight on Tim's face.

Brian was a skinny guy in jeans and an untucked Rolling Stones T-shirt. This was the same Brian who had let his camera go out of focus in San Diego. Although Uncle Mike had gotten angry over Brian's carelessness, it was the first time Brian had messed up. He'd been with Uncle Mike for years, and normally he was one of the best cameramen around. Uncle Mike was sure he wouldn't make the same mistake again.

Uncle Mike had the rest of his crew shooting the race itself. Later, in the postproduction edit, we would use the PR man's comments in voice-over to tie the segments together.

I stood near Tim Becker, listening as the race continued. Out there on the track, the cars were a blur of color. I kept my camera on Tim's face, but I did it from a weird angle.

He ignored me, just like everyone else did. That was the great thing about being so young. No one—except Uncle Mike—figured I could do anything of value. It let me be just like a fly on the wall, listening and watching and nearly invisible.

"Races are won and lost on pit stops," Tim Becker was saying. "Sandy stays in close contact with the crew on her radio. They try to make the best decision possible on when to bring her in."

I looked over at George Lot. His tall body was frozen as he gave total concentration to the race. I got a quick shot of him, then turned back to Tim Becker. His face looked square in my viewfinder.

"Right now," Tim said, "even if the pit stop is only twenty seconds long, it might cost her half a lap or more. She's in fourth place. A pit stop might move her back to tenth. If the pit crew is a few seconds slower than it should be, she might drop back to fifteenth."

I glanced up at a television monitor that showed the network coverage being broadcast to millions of viewers. I decided to film that. I zoomed in and zoomed out.

Twenty laps into the race, Sandy was part of a tight pack of cars. There were five of them, almost bumper to bumper. She jockeyed down on the track, trying to get beneath the third-place car as they all came out of a turn. She wasn't able to make it though, and she had to slide back in behind again.

"The best thing possible for her would be a yellow flag," Tim said. "She'd be able to come in, fuel up and change tires without losing her place. Trouble is, so would all the other leaders, so she wouldn't gain on them."

My eyes were still on the monitor as Tim spoke. Yellow flag. I flicked my mind through the research I had done. It's the caution flag that comes out when an accident or something makes the track dangerous.

I said that into my camera's microphone. Then I shut my mouth so I could pick up more of Tim's commentary.

"At this part of the race," Tim said, "a pit stop decision is not as crucial as it becomes toward the end. Everybody has to come in at least once before the end, so even if Sandy comes in under a green flag, she knows most others will have to as well. She'll regain her place on them. Unless..."

On the monitor, the cars seemed to move slowly. But that was because the camera panned the track with them, so the background moved instead. But if the camera were fixed on one spot, the cars would flash by quicker than an eyeblink.

Tim had paused halfway into his sentence because he too had looked up at the monitor. Sandy darted downward on the track again at the end of a turn.

"She's caught his draft!" Tim said. "She's making it past!"

Draft. I knew what that was too. The drivers stayed as close behind the leader as they could to stay in the draft of the lead car as it cut through the air. Every car behind had less air to cut through. It could help them go another five miles an hour faster.

"She's in third place," Tim hollered. "And moving into second!"

Sure enough, she was using the draft of the second-place car to slingshot ahead.

George Lot had not moved. If he was happy with what was happening, nothing about him showed it.

This was good stuff. If we could contrast Tim's excitement with George's professionalism, viewers would love it. I moved my camera back and forth.

"All right," Tim said. "From what I can see, here's the situation. She might have another five laps left on her tires. And maybe seven laps of gasoline. But her pit crew knows the distance better than she does. If they think she's going to lose a tire, they'll call her in. But they'll want to wait as long as possible, hoping for a yellow flag. The worst thing that could happen is to have her come in under a green flag, lose a lap and then two laps later get a yellow so that everyone else can refuel without losing any time."

Tim took a deep breath. "Second place," he said. "This is awesome. If she can keep it there without losing a tire, or a motor, or running into someone else's accident, or seeing any trouble in the pit..."

I was beginning to understand why everybody was so keyed up every single second of a three-hour race. Even if Sandy looked like she had it made, there were a hundred things that could go wrong.

"So now it's a waiting game," Tim said. "She's got to run every lap at this same pace, not a split second less. And she's got to keep doing it as long as possible, hoping for a yellow, even if it means staying out there on her final six ounces of fuel."

Six ounces. Less than a can of soda. And this was in a car that was burning a gallon every two laps.

I felt a strange excitement. I realized I was getting caught up in the race. I gave myself a mental slap across the face. I couldn't ever be a good director if I let my emotions get involved with my subject.

As I forced my excitement to cool down, I glanced back at Tim Becker. His eyes were on the monitor. A red flush covered his face. His voice was growing higher in pitch.

"Okay," he said, "this is what she has to watch out for as she comes into the pit. If there's a yellow flag, there will be a traffic jam as thirty cars all come in at once. If it's a green, she's got to start slowing down in turn four and drop to the bottom of the track to approach pit road. She's got to get in and out as fast as possible, but if she's even a half mile an hour over fifty-five, she'll break the pit road speed limit, and she'll get a black flag."

Black flag. That means the driver has to return to the pit for a stop-and-go penalty—waiting those endless seconds while the chances of getting back to the lead get smaller and smaller.

"And she's got to stop right on the mark," Tim said. "If she overshoots the pit, she'll have to back up. That can cost more valuable seconds."

I walked around Brian Nelson to see what he was getting through his camera. If the light gave a good angle, the red flush of excitement on Tim's face would show up clearly and give more to this segment. Standing at an angle behind Brian, I shot some of Brian's camera and Tim Becker.

I frowned.

Brian's camera light was not on.

How could he see anything through the viewfinder if the camera wasn't on?

I tapped him on the shoulder. I pointed at the dull light.

His jaw dropped. "Sorry, man," he said. "I just got so caught up in watching the race that I stopped paying attention to my viewfinder."

And at that moment, the roar of a hundred and fifty thousand people was so loud that he snapped his head back toward the track.

It snapped me back to the track too. Along with my handheld. I had the viewfinder so glued to my eye that it was just like another part of my body.

I saw that in front of us, a car was spinning out of control. Another car slammed into its back end. Then another.

Three other cars zoomed by. They all separated so quickly that the next car didn't see the stopped cars until the very last second.

Into my viewfinder came the next car. Red. Scarlet red. Sandy Peterson's car. And she had less than a heartbeat to react to the accident.

chapter ten

I kept filming.

Sandy swung her wheel hard. Her front fender clipped the back end of the car in front of her. She plowed ahead, smoke rising from her tires. She fought for control and somehow swung the Chevy down to the bottom of the track. Still going, still smoking, she headed toward pit road.

Yellow flag!

Sandy was closest to pit road. Her speed was down. Way down.

She gunned the motor and the car strained to push forward against the tire that burned against the fender.

More smoke.

More squealing tires.

And she was headed right toward us.

I took my camera away from my eyes so I could look where I was going as I got out of the way.

I saw that Brian Nelson was watching the action with his mouth hanging open.

"Shoot this!" I shouted. Uncle Mike was too busy juggling the in-car cameras and audio to notice that Brian was doing nothing. "Shoot this!"

I swung my camera around toward the car.

"Tim!" I shouted as I searched for the action through my viewfinder. "Give me audio. Keep talking. Give us the play-by-play."

My camera would catch the action and his words. Later, we could patch everything together. Now I just needed to record as much as possible.

The back end of the Chevy swung crazily back and forth as Sandy fought to control a skid.

She brought the car in perfectly. And I had it all on film.

As George barked orders, eight crew members shot forward. One of them pushed a giant jack under the car.

"She caught a break," Tim said. He spoke quickly, urgently. "This yellow flag lets her come in without losing time to the other drivers. She's looking at a minute, maybe two minutes in the pit for her crew to fix the damage she just got. That could have put her down maybe three laps under a green flag."

The Chevy was already off the ground. Four men attacked the tires.

With a couple of high-speed screams from their air guns, the single giant bolt on each tire released. Other crew members were ready to pull the tires off and throw new ones on—except for the front right tire where the front fender was pushed in against the still-smoking tire.

"Move it with the hammers!" George shouted. "Move it! Move it! Move it!"

Two of the crew jumped forward, pounding with big hammers to knock the fender back off the tire. As soon as the fender released, the fourth tire fell loose. Another two crew members hoisted the new tire into place.

In the back of the car, they'd already finished pouring twenty gallons of fuel into the car. While all of this was happening, someone was mopping Sandy's face with a cool wet cloth.

"It's been forty-five seconds," Tim said. "On the track, they've pushed the cars down and cleared the wreck."

I checked the main television monitor, filming it as I did. All three cars were off the track. The drivers had pulled themselves out of their cars. One kicked the ground. The other two walked away with their shoulders slumped.

I swung my camera back to the Scarlet Thunder. Sandy was just swinging the visor of her helmet down.

All the crew cleared the car.

She roared ahead, just beating another car coming down pit road behind her.

Then I noticed the crew had drawn into a circle. Someone was down in the middle.

I stepped closer, filming, filming, filming.

One of the crew, a little red-headed guy, was squirming in agony. I could see him clutching his knee.

"He got bounced with a hammer," someone explained. "Took him down like he'd been shot."

I closed in on the guy's face. Our television viewers were going to love how real this was.

"You guys are vampires," I heard a voice say. "Real vampires."

That came from George Lot.

"Huh?" I said. I didn't stop filming my close-up. "Vampires?"

"That man is flesh and blood. He's in agony. And all you can think about is the camera shot?"

Without shifting my camera, I gave him the answer I'd heard Uncle Mike give dozens of times. "We didn't hurt him. We're not part of it."

"You would be if you were human," George said.

Before I could argue, his radio squawked.

He walked away.

That left me standing there. Alone.

What does he know about our job? I asked myself. Nothing.

I zoomed back from the hurt pit crew member and got a wide angle of the people helping him walk away.

chapter eleven

That night, long after the race had ended, Uncle Mike and I watched it from Sandy Peterson's point of view.

That had been Uncle Mike's job—juggling Sandy's audio and the cameras that showed the front and rear views.

We sat back in the darkness of a motel room as we reviewed those segments.

After the yellow flag that let the crew repair her dinged front fender, Sandy had reentered the track.

The front camera had a view from the dash. It showed the pavement in a blur coming toward her. The rear camera, mounted with a view through the back window, showed the pit crew growing smaller behind her, with another race car slowly filling the view.

Then she entered the track.

"I'm looking to get back in line," she said into her audio. "I wish the yellow-flag restart was more like Indy Car."

Uncle Mike put the video on pause and asked me to explain. I told him what I knew from all the studying I had done earlier. The Indy Car Formula racers in their low-slung sleek cars, unlike stock cars, had a much easier time restarting. Indy Car rules put all the cars in single file with the lead-lap cars mixed in with the lapped cars, in the order they came out of the pit.

In stock-car racing, leaders were allowed to bunch up for a restart, with the cars that are down a lap lined up single file to the inside of the leaders. That meant Sandy, as one of the leaders, would be in a big pack of cars when the race began again.

Sure enough, the front and back cameras showed cars moving in on her. The cameras gave a wide-angle view that distorted the bumpers of those cars. Still, it was accurate enough to make you almost feel like you were there.

"Come on, boys," Sandy said in her mike, "give me your best shot."

I grinned. That would be a good voice-over to splice into the finished documentary.

Restart!

Sandy's audio picked up the swelling roar of a couple of dozen 750-horsepower engines all gunning it together.

Another great audio clip.

Then the ducking and weaving and fighting for position began all over again.

Her front camera showed that she almost drove onto the trunk of the car in front of her. Her rear camera showed one car on each side, both of those almost banging her bumper.

And this was at 180 miles per hour.

"Heat's bad," Sandy said to audio. "It's like sitting in a sauna for three hours. Not only that—"

She stopped.

"Hang on," she said calmly. "I see day-light."

I didn't. All I saw in her front-view camera was rushing pavement and the spoilers of the two cars ahead.

She swerved, and then I saw it. But it didn't look like enough room. Then the car on the right gave way, and she was through.

"That was a paint-scraper," she said. "It—"

Again, she stopped short. A car was coming up behind her fast on the left-hand side. The camera showed her going high into a corner. She moved slightly left, the car behind her backed off.

Then she was through the corner, coming out low.

She drifted high again, almost kissing the concrete wall. The pavement and concrete were moving so fast that I could not imagine the concentration it took to stay in place.

The silence over the next half hour showed exactly how much concentration it took. She had warned us before the race that talking to our audio system would be the last thing on her mind. The race and her pit crew were more important.

Not that there was total silence.

Every half lap or so we could hear George on her radio.

"How do the tires feel?" he asked.

"Hot," she said. "But I don't want to give anything up going into the corners. Not when we worked so hard to get us here."

"Pushing hard enough to squeal?" he asked.

"This isn't my first race," she answered.

Another voice took me away from the race.

I realized it was Uncle Mike. Asking me to hit Pause.

"Tire squeal?" he asked.

"You know the answer, don't you," I said, grinning. "This is a test."

He nodded. "Pass it."

I thought it over. "All right. Once tires get over two hundred and twenty-five degrees, they lose grip. As they lose grip, they slide and get even hotter. Squealing is the fastest way to let you know you're pushing too hard."

"A-plus," Uncle Mike said, matching my grin. "Let's get back to the race."

We watched another five laps. Again, all I could do was shake my head in admiration. The front and back camera views showed how much skill it took to stay on the track at those high speeds. She was still silent, intent on keeping her second-place position.

George's voice broke in. "Are you losing speed on the straights?"

"Don't seem to be. Worried about the bodywork?" she replied.

I hit Pause on the video playback.

"I asked one of the crew about the new fender they banged into place," I said to Uncle Mike. "Actually, I did more than ask. I filmed one of the guys. He told me that their biggest worry was spoiling the air flow. He said banged-up bumpers and crumpled fenders were as much a part of stock-car racing as hot dogs and cola in the stands. A few dents won't slow a car, but any major fender damage will cause air drag above one hundred and forty miles per hour. If they did a bad job, it might cost her ten miles an hour in speed."

I hit Play on the video again, catching her voice as she went into the straights.

"The crew did a great job," she said. "No vibration, no shake. I feel good about this race."

She should have. She finished fourth.

Fourth might have made her happy, but it didn't do much for us. Because we didn't get it on film.

Ten seconds later, in the hotel room where we sat, the television screen went black. We figured out later that someone had loaded nearly dead batteries into all the equipment.

chapter twelve

We were two weeks behind our shooting schedule.

We had traveled to a different track for a different race. Concord, North Carolina. But it still looked the same, because all I really saw was either a hotel room or an infield track with stands in the background.

It was the night before qualifying runs. The Scarlet Thunder crew had invited the film crew to a barbecue on the infield, in front of the motor homes. A storm had passed by earlier, clearing the air of heat and humidity.

I looked around the gathered crowd. I saw Brian Nelson and Margaret Lynn, another camera person. Ken Takarura, a famous sports interviewer, sat with Uncle Mike. Mike had flown Ken in for the weekend to interview Sandy Peterson. Al Simonsen, who was in charge of audio, hovered nearby.

Tim Becker had joined us too. Sandy had gone back to her hotel room to try to get as much rest as possible. So Tim, as public relations man, had been assigned to stay with us to answer any and all questions. He was pleased we had accepted the invitation to enjoy this family-style barbecue with the crew instead of eating at a restaurant somewhere. I was too, because I had a huge steak on the grill that smelled great.

I was also filming with my handheld camera. People had long stopped joking about the camera as a growth on my shoulder. Now they just went about their business and left me alone. I got a few minutes of footage of the crew standing around talking and laughing. Then I turned the camera to Uncle Mike.

He was talking to Tim Becker about Sandy's most recent crash during this week's practice runs. A crash that I had caught myself with my handheld. I felt real good about the footage; the flames and smoke would look pretty dramatic on television.

"We weren't that worried about her being hurt," Tim said. "She slid off the wall and didn't have any real impact. Besides, the drivers wear special fire-retardant suits. She was out of the car right away, and the fire crew had the flames smothered in about thirty seconds."

"Did Sandy say how she lost control?" Uncle Mike asked. I kept filming, moving my camera onto his face. "I mean, she's a great driver. She can qualify in her sleep. Why would she hit the wall with no one else on the track?"

"Loose rear wheel," Tim said. "She says it wouldn't quite hold the turn."

Tim turned to me. He smiled into the camera. "Remember, Trenton, even though you've got that on film, Sandy won't let you air it on television. Can you imagine what the press would do with it? Can you imagine the headline? Crew Fails To Check Car. That wouldn't be good for the team. Or the sponsor. And we need to keep the sponsor happy."

I nodded from behind my camera.

"If you shut that off," he said, "I'll tell you more."

I lowered the camera but let it run. I angled it upward from my hip, hoping he wouldn't notice.

"You see," he continued, "in my business, you always have to worry about appearances. A rumor like that could really hurt the team. Besides, Sandy might have been looking for an excuse. She hit the wall pretty hard. That alone is enough to loosen any wheel."

"But if she's a good driver," I said, "wouldn't she feel when something's wrong? She does know what she's talking about, right?"

"Of course, of course," he said quickly. Almost like he didn't believe it. Almost like he was a public relations person whose first thought was always to say the right thing. "Sandy is one of the best. The whole team believes in her."

He said that too, like it was something he was automatically supposed to say. I remembered Sandy telling me and Uncle Mike how much she needed to win a race soon or she wouldn't be driving much longer.

I hoped my camera had kept Tim in the viewfinder frame. This was great stuff, even if he didn't want me filming it.

I didn't feel guilty about trying to catch him on film either. Good directors didn't let anything or anyone stop them from getting the very best work possible.

The only thing that got me to set my camera down in the next few minutes was my steak, medium rare. And, of course, I had to take another short break for dessert.

"This is George Lot's specialty," Tim Becker said as he came back with dessert dishes for the film crew. "He makes it every week for these barbecues. He uses at least a dozen different types of fruits and berries. Always fresh. And healthy too. Except for the sweet whipped cream he folds into them."

"No, thanks," Margaret Lynn said. She was in her twenties. Uncle Mike thought she was great behind the camera; she often caught unusual angles. She'd pulled her long dark hair into a braid and wore a *Save the Whales* T-shirt. She was also a vegetarian and had chosen to eat a huge salad for her meal. "I don't generally eat dairy products. And that whipped cream looks too rich."

Like everyone else, I dug into my bowl of fruit, enjoying the tangy flavors and sweet creaminess as the conversation continued around me.

I listened as Brian Nelson and Al Simonsen picked up a long-running argument they had with Margaret Lynn. Brian and Al had long hair and each wore a single earring. They, however, were wearing *Nuke the Whales* T-shirts. Not that they wanted whales to be nuked, but they loved doing anything that raised Margaret's blood pressure.

And now they were arguing that we didn't need farmers because everyone knew we could just get food from grocery stores.

I laughed at Margaret's expression as I finished my fruit and picked up my camera.

Ken Takarura sat quietly beside me and just listened as he ate. Ken was older, with fine gray hair and a thick gray goatee. He wore tiny, round glasses and looked the part he would play in our documentary: an intelligent interviewer unafraid of the difficult questions.

"So, Tim," Uncle Mike said between bites of his dessert, "Sandy managed to qualify in spite of her crash. It seems like a banged-up car and blown engine could have kept her out of racing for about a month."

The PR man shook his head. "A racing team is just that. A team. About thirty people. Engineers. Mechanics. Administration. There are two guys who just rebuild extra motors. Another two guys who can replace a motor almost as fast as some people can make a sandwich."

I'd gotten all of that with my camera.

"In fact," Tim said, "there's not much trouble that this team can't lick."

"Same with my team," Uncle Mike said. "This crew can handle anything."

Except for what happened to us very, very early the next morning.

chapter thirteen

For me, it started with a bad dream. I was in a swamp. The water was up to my waist. My feet were stuck in mud. I watched an alligator swim through the waving grass in the water. It got closer. I couldn't run because my feet would not move. The jaws opened wide. I screamed. The jaws closed on my stomach.

The pain was so real that I woke up.

I blinked for a few seconds, expecting to still be in a swamp.

I wasn't.

I was in a rented motor home that I shared with Uncle Mike. We had decided to spend this week living like the pit crew and filming them in their everyday activities. So we too were parked in the infield among the dozens and dozens of other motor homes that housed the different racing crews. The rest of the film crew was in a motor home parked beside ours.

Still blinking, I was rattled by how real the dream had seemed. So rattled that it took me a couple more seconds to realize the alligator was still clamped on my stomach. Except, of course, there was no alligator.

I had stomach cramps. Real bad stomach cramps. So bad that I heard groaning, and it didn't even feel like it was coming from my mouth.

When I heard the groaning again, I realized that it came from another part of the motor home. The part where Uncle Mike slept.

I looked at the clock beside my bed. The red glowing numbers showed 1:30 AM.

My stomach cramps got worse. I groaned too. I almost felt like I was going to throw up.

I heard Uncle Mike get out of his bed.

I didn't say anything. I was afraid that if I tried to talk, all my insides would come out of my mouth in a big explosion.

Uncle Mike staggered through the motor home in the darkness. I heard a bang.

"Nuts!" he said. Probably his toe. There was a step in the motor home that I had already hit twice.

Uncle Mike hopped around.

So did my stomach.

It hopped and flopped. I got that feeling you get when you know you're going to blow. The feeling that says you have exactly 2.5 seconds until the geyser hits. The feeling that says you had better use those 2.5 seconds to get someplace other than the bed where you are lying beneath the covers.

I bolted upright. I hit my head on the low ceiling.

In the darkness, I saw an awesome display of circles of light. But my head hurt so bad

I didn't feel like applauding. And my body was already in full motion.

I shoulder-checked Uncle Mike, who was still hopping. He fell across the table. I didn't stop to apologize. I was down to 1.5 seconds.

I ripped open the bathroom door. I fell to my knees in front of the toilet.

As I was throwing up, I became aware that not all of the horrible sounds were mine.

Uncle Mike was using the sink to do the same thing.

It just made me throw up harder.

After what felt like five years of agony, there was nothing left in my stomach. About two pounds of steak and whipped cream and fresh fruit had just gone to waste.

I didn't feel any better though. Most times it is a relief to throw up. Not this time. I still felt dizzy and could hardly breathe.

In the darkness of the bathroom, I pushed past Uncle Mike as he leaned over the sink.

"Air," I croaked. "I need air."

I got to the motor home door. Because it was so dark, it took what felt like five years for me to figure out how to open the lock. It was five years filled with a stomach still in the grip of an alligator, lungs that were pushing against a giant vise, and hands and arms that hardly obeyed what I told them to do.

Finally, I snapped open the lock, flipped the door open and half fell getting outside.

The air was hot compared to the cool air-conditioned air inside of the trailer.

It didn't matter. At least I had room around me.

I sat on a lawn chair.

What was happening to me? My body was shaking. I could still hardly breathe. And my stomach hurt so bad I wanted to cry.

Then I heard the same sound I had heard inside our motor home.

The sound of someone throwing up. Except this time it was someone outside. Someone nearby.

I strained my eyes. There was just enough light for me to see Brian Nelson, our cameraman, and Ken Takarura, the interviewer.

They were both outside the rented motor home they shared with Al Simonsen. Brian and Ken were bent over and heaving in a horrible way.

Uncle Mike staggered outside to join me. He stood in front of me, leaning on his knees and gasping for breath.

All he could do was groan.

Brian and Ken kept throwing up.

They were so loud that lights began to come on in trailers nearby.

"Hey!" someone yelled. "Keep it down out there!"

That warning didn't mean a thing. Brian and Ken retched even louder.

"Look, you guys, if you don't stop that noise, I'm going to come out there!" the voice shouted.

"Knock off the shouting!" another person shouted. "We need sleep here."

More lights flipped on. More shouting echoed through the infield.

It might have been funny. But I couldn't focus on anything except my stomach. It began to flip again.

"Uncle Mike," I said, hardly above a whisper. My heart was racing hard. "I think I'm going to..."

I had thought my stomach was totally empty. I was wrong. Very wrong. I knew because of how much covered Uncle Mike's legs before he moved out of my way.

When I finished, I fell over.

I lay there with my heart pounding, gasping until an emergency crew finally arrived. Strong hands lifted me onto a stretcher and put me into an ambulance, with Uncle Mike beside me.

As my vision got darker and blurrier, the ambulance took us away into the night.

chapter fourteen

"Dizziness, headache, vomiting." The white-coated doctor in front of us made notes on his clipboard as he spoke. His name tag said *Dr. Ellroy*. "Stomach cramps, breathing difficulties."

"Yes," Uncle Mike groaned. "I wish I didn't have to agree, but yes."

The two of us shared a hospital room. Down the hall, Brian Nelson, Ken Takarura and Al Simonsen shared another room, waiting for their turn to see the same doctor.

Al was the reason the other two had been throwing up outside. Al had been in the motor home's bathroom.

"Gastroenteritis and tachycardia," Dr. Ellroy said, more to himself than to us.

"Huh?" I groaned.

The doctor looked up from his clipboard. Although he was young, his square face sagged from exhaustion. I didn't blame him. The clock on the hospital wall behind him showed almost three o'clock. He was an internal specialist and had been paged from his home.

"Gastroenteritis is an inflammation of the stomach and bowels. It causes stomach cramping and diarrhea. Have either of you had diarrhea yet?"

"Yet?" I said.

Uncle Mike's white face got even whiter. "Doc," he said, "why did you have to put that into my mind?"

"I'm not trying to put anything into your mind. It's just that—"

"The bathroom, Doc," Uncle Mike groaned. "Where's the bathroom?"

Dr. Ellroy pointed at the door. "Down the hallway to your left."

Uncle Mike got off the edge of the bed where he'd been sitting. He hobbled out the door.

I swallowed. It hurt. My throat was raw.

"That other word," I said. "Tacky... tacky..."

"Tachycardia. A faster than normal heart-beat."

The doctor looked down at his clipboard again. "Dizziness. Headache. Vomiting. Stomach cramps. Breathing difficulties. Gastroenteritis. Tachycardia."

Dr. Ellroy's eyes came back up at me again. "Anything else?"

"I was shaking. Bad."

He made another note on his clipboard.

He tapped his front teeth with his pencil. "I'm guessing the three in the other room had the same symptoms."

"Probably," I said. I had been too busy throwing up to take notes on anyone else.

"Then it's definitely some type of poisoning," he said.

"Poisoning?!"

Dr. Ellroy smiled. "Not like in a movie kind of poisoning where a bad guy was trying to kill you. More like food poisoning. Still, this is pretty serious. We need to track it down. So let me ask you the obvious question. Were all of you in a place where you ate the same food?"

I nodded as I thought about the barbecue. What was weird was that no one from the pit crew had joined us. Almost as if only Uncle Mike's crew had been poisoned.

"We were at a barbecue," I said. "We—"

I stopped as a scary thought hit me.

"Yes?" The doctor prompted.

"Margaret Lynn!" I said. "She was with us too! She's staying at a motel! What if she's real sick and no one knows it?"

Without any hesitation, Dr. Ellroy pulled a small cell phone from his coat pocket. He snapped it open.

"What motel?" he asked.

"The...the..." I struggled to remember. We had dropped her off after the barbecue because she wanted some privacy. She didn't want to share the motor home the rest of the film crew used. I tried to picture the neon sign against the night sky: *Riverside Motel*.

He punched a few numbers and waited. "Yes," he said. "I need the number for the Riverside Motel."

After a few more seconds of waiting, he punched in more numbers. And waited briefly again.

"Yes," he said. "I would like to speak to a guest registered at the motel."

He gave me a questioning look.

"Margaret Lynn," I said.

"Margaret Lynn," he repeated into the cell phone.

For the next few seconds, I again felt stuck in mud with an alligator swimming closer. What if she had passed out? This was some kind of poisoning. What if she had...

"Hello," Doctor Ellroy said into the phone. "This is Doctor John Ellroy. I'm an internal specialist and I—"

He closed his eyes. Even I could hear how loud Margaret Lynn was yelling into the telephone.

"No," Dr. Ellroy said. "This is not Al or Brian. This is not a practical joke. I am calling because we were afraid that you might be ill. However, you sound very healthy and strong. I am sorry to have bothered you."

He snapped the phone shut. He smiled. "It didn't seem the time for a long conversation."

He began tapping his teeth again with his pencil. "This could help," he said. "It could help a lot. Was there anything you all ate that she did not?"

"She's a vegetarian," I said. "Does that help?"

"Perhaps."

I snapped my fingers. "No," I said. "Dessert. We all had a fruit dessert with whipped cream. She didn't. But Tim Becker, another guy who sat with us, did."

Doctor Ellroy made a couple more phone calls and finally reached Tim Becker. Doctor Ellroy spoke seriously with him for a few minutes, then hung up.

"As you could tell from our conversation," Dr. Ellroy said, "he's sick too, though he doesn't sound as bad off as you are. I'd say it's a safe bet you're all reacting to the dessert."

Doctor Ellroy frowned. "The strange thing here is that the symptoms sound like something that commonly happens to children who pick and eat raw elderberries."

"Elderberries?" I echoed.

"Yes," he said. "Cooked elderberries are fine. But uncooked, they'll cause exactly what you've experienced. The symptoms won't kill you, but they will slow you down. Raw elderberries contain a poison called cyanogenic glycoside."

I didn't care much about the name of the poison. I cared much more about a bigger question. One that Dr. Ellroy asked out loud for both of us. Especially after I explained that only Uncle Mike's crew had been poisoned.

"But why," he said, "would someone put raw elderberries in selective desserts?"

Before either of us could try to answer, a new kind of rumbling hit my insides. Not the throwing-up kind of rumbling. But the kind of rumbling that had sent Uncle Mike out the door in a big hurry.

"Um, Doctor Ellroy?" I said.

"Yes?"

I was already running out the door as I answered.

"Got to go," I said.

And I meant it in the truest way. I sprinted down the hall, looking for a bathroom.

Stupid elderberries.

chapter fifteen

Those stupid elderberries cost us nearly a full day of production, setting us even further behind Uncle Mike's million-dollar deadline.

Since it was the day between Friday's qualifying and Sunday's race, the original plan had been to interview Sandy in the morning and film the pit crew in the afternoon.

We'd canceled the pit crew film segments because we needed several cameras for those. Brian Nelson was still too sick to work. Margaret Lynn, though, was fine. So even though we couldn't shoot using the two-angle method, Uncle Mike decided to go ahead with Ken Takarura's interview with Sandy Peterson.

He chose to interview Sandy in one of the motor homes. The backdrop was a simple black sheet. Sandy wore jeans and a light blue polo shirt. Uncle Mike wanted her to look pretty, but not too feminine, and together they had decided the light blue would do the trick.

I intended to keep my camera running the whole time.

Sandy sat on a cane-backed chair with Ken Takarura beside her. He wasn't in the best shape. We hid the sick whiteness of his face with good lighting and lots of stage makeup. I had a bottle of fizzy water for him to drink off-camera between his questions.

I didn't feel so great either. But I knew the deadline was too important to miss, and if Uncle Mike could force himself to work, so could I.

Not that this was something I would call work.

I was having fun.

Ken began the interview by paying Sandy some compliments. He wanted her to be relaxed so that he could catch her off guard with a tough question. Hopefully, she would be surprised and it would show on camera. Later, we would cut out the first part, so that at the beginning, viewers saw only the question and her answer.

"Yes," Ken was saying in his deep voice. "At those speeds, the slightest mistake will put you out of the race. You need total concentration on the track, don't you?"

"More than total," Sandy answered. She smiled. I was watching the television monitor hooked up to the camera. With her blond hair and soft features, she was interesting to watch. Especially with what she did for a living. "Ken, you can't let your lap times be more than a tenth of a second off your pace. Think of it. A typical race is four hundred laps. If you lose a tenth of a second every third or fourth lap, that's..."

She bit her front lip as she paused to do her math. I was doing it at the same time. Say every fourth lap equals one hundred laps. Then one hundred times a tenth of a second would be...

"Ten seconds," she said. "That may not sound like much, but in ten seconds at the speeds we travel, that might put you back by a half lap by the end of the race. I can't tell you how many races are lost by the length of a car."

She smiled into the camera again. "And Ken, it's not just the time you have to worry about. You need to keep your concentration focused, because if you daydream for a heartbeat, or blink at the wrong time, you can hit the wall or another car. It's not like driving through town to pick up groceries."

Ken nodded. I knew he was about to spring the question that Uncle Mike had planned. And this was probably the best time.

"That brings me to something else," Ken said. "Aren't you afraid of dying?"

The question hung there. How many people, after all, like to talk about their own death?

"Funny you should ask," she said. The camera caught every twitch of every muscle on her face. We had expected to surprise her, but her face looked calm. "I think about dying every time I get behind the wheel."

"Do other drivers?" Ken asked.

"I can't speak for other drivers," she said.

Great answer, I thought. She was a pro at interviews.

"But for yourself..." Ken was a pro too.

"For myself," she answered, "I'm ready to die. Don't get me wrong. I don't want to. At least not before I have to."

Another smile. "There's this saying: 'Don't do the crime, if you can't do the time.' In other words, be sure you're ready for the price you'll have to pay if you get caught."

"Interesting...," Ken said.

"When I get into a racecar," she continued, "I would be foolish if I wasn't ready to pay the price for making a mistake.

And, in this sport, a mistake can kill you. It doesn't happen too often, because the cars and tracks are set up to reduce that risk, but it does happen."

"So tell me," Ken said, "what makes you so ready to accept death?"

She smiled again. This was going to be a great interview segment. Tough questions and unafraid answers.

"The long view."

"The long view?" Ken asked. She had him hooked. And if she had him hooked, people watching the documentary would be hooked too.

"Sure," she said. "Do you believe in God?"

She had caught Ken off guard. And he was supposed to be the interviewer.

"Do you believe in God?" she repeated. "Surveys show that up to seventy percent of people believe in God."

"Well...," he said.

"What I find amazing," she said, showing us the tough Sandy Peterson who stood up for what she believed in, "is what people will discuss on television in front of millions of people—weird things, private things, stupid things. All stuff that should embarrass them. But it doesn't. Then ask someone about God like I did just now..."

Ken squirmed. Uncle Mike, though, was too good a director to stop the camera now. He'd cut out the stuff that made Ken look bad and use bits and pieces of what Sandy was saying. I'd vote for keeping most of what she said. She was right, after all, about television. I'd seen some of those talk shows.

"Anyway," Sandy said, "if you don't believe in God, death is pretty scary. Because then that's all there is. But if you believe that He is waiting, it is a lot easier to feel confident about getting into a racecar..."

She stopped for a moment, thinking about her audience. "And this isn't just about racecar drivers. Think about all the car accidents that happen away from the race-track. Anybody anywhere who gets behind a steering wheel, especially teenagers, because they don't have as much driving experience, should think about what I'm saying..."

Ken coughed quietly. I quickly handed him a drink off-camera, then stepped back.

The liquid helped him recover his voice quickly. He was about to ask another question when George Lot burst into the motor home.

"Sandy," he said. The big crew chief held a folded newspaper in his right hand. He waved it at her.

"George," she said, without getting up. "We're in the middle of something."

"I know," he said, "but you're going to want to see this. Tim Becker just called me about it. He said he's starting to feel better and would come to the track later. But he's crazy mad. He asked me to show this to you. He wants to scrap the whole film shoot. The rest of the crew just want to quit."

"What?!?" Sandy stood up. She took the newspaper from her crew chief.

"Driver Blames Crew," she read from the headline. "Loose rear wheel leads to crash during practice run."

George nodded. "When you read the rest, you'll see that an inside source is quoted.

And that inside source is named as someone from a television film crew."

He looked at Uncle Mike and glared. I was happy that George did not have a big wrench in his hand.

Sandy quickly scanned the rest of the article.

I remembered what Tim Becker had said during the barbecue: "Remember, Trenton, even though you've got that on film, Sandy won't let you air it on television. Can you imagine what the press would do with it? Can you imagine the headline? Crew Fails To Check Car. That wouldn't be good for the team. Or the sponsor. And we need to keep the sponsor happy."

When she finished reading, Sandy Peterson looked straight at Uncle Mike.

"What I'd like to say," she told him, "is that you're finished. That this whole film thing is over. That you should get out, now."

She took a deep breath. "But I long ago promised myself to fight my temper. So I'll say this instead..."

We waited as she chose her words. Her blue eyes flashed.

"This interview is over. I want time to cool down. And I'll give you some time to clear yourself. But if you can't prove to me that I shouldn't blame you for this, I'll have to ask you to pack up."

chapter sixteen

Alone in Uncle Mike's motor home, I sat facing the television and playback unit. I had expected to spend part of the morning reviewing the film from my handheld camera. But I was too depressed. I set it aside without bothering to look at any of it.

I had worked hours and hours, wandering around and filming by myself because I had believed this would be my first chance to get credit on a big project. Instead, it looked like all of those hours of film were going to be a wasted effort.

It didn't even help when I reminded myself how much worse it was for Uncle Mike. Through the window, I watched him pace around outside with his cell phone. He was too upset to sit still as he called Hollywood. I knew he was trying to sell his script. He couldn't figure out how to prove who had spoken with the press. He fully expected Sandy to call off the shoot. Without Sandy's agreement to film, there was no way he could make his deadline. Uncle Mike needed to sell his script for as much money as he could, even though he would lose ownership control of one of the hottest projects in Hollywood.

I had merely lost all those hours of filming. Uncle Mike had lost more than a million dollars. And all because of a series of dumb things that had happened since the beginning of the shoot. Or even before the shoot, if I counted how much time we lost because of Junior Louis and the mice.

I stared at the blank television screen.

I was thinking too much. I didn't want to think. And the best way to not work your brain is to watch television.

So I grabbed the remote from beside me and clicked it on. I began to flick through channels. Uncle Mike had rented a motor home with a satellite dish. There were a lot of channels.

I saw a *Bugs Bunny* cartoon.

Great, I told myself, now even television wasn't letting me escape. *Bugs Bunny* reminded me of the cartoon where the elephant was scared of a mouse. And that, of course, reminded me of Junior Louis all over again. I even remembered telling the trainer about the cartoon and mice and—

Stop! I thought. What else did the trainer say that morning?

I closed my eyes and frowned, thinking as hard as I could. I pictured myself standing beside the elephant. I imagined how it smelled. I listened hard to my voice in my memory. And then I remembered exactly how the conversation had gone.

What about mice? Does Junior Louis get excited about mice? You know, like in the old *Bugs Bunny* cartoon?

Those had been my questions. The trainer had laughed.

I've seen that cartoon too, he'd said. It's funny, you're the second person to ask me that today.

I repeated that phrase in my mind: It's funny, you're the second person to ask me that today. I snapped off the television and stared at the blank screen again. I thought hard. What if that first person had asked for a reason? Like to find out if mice really would bother Junior Louis. Like to find out if it would be worthwhile to put mice in the cooler.

I needed to find a telephone and call the trainer. He would be easy to reach— I knew he worked with the elephants at the San Diego Zoo. But Uncle Mike was using his cell phone. And I'd forgotten to charge mine. It was dead.

I needed to find a pay phone. Except the nearest pay phone I could remember was in the stands. Across the track. I thought hard about whether there was a closer one.

Then it hit me. Tim Becker had a phone in his public relations trailer. He would probably let me use it.

I got up in a hurry. I was on a mission.

chapter seventeen

In the late morning sunshine, I began to walk between the trailers and cars and other motor homes toward Tim Becker's trailer. It didn't take me long to get there.

The screen door to the trailer was closed, but the inner door was open. I heard classical music playing inside.

I knocked.

"Come in," Tim said.

I opened the door.

"Hi," I said.

"What can I do for you?" he asked. I could tell he was still mad about the newspaper article. But, ever the public relations man, Tim was polite. He sat behind a desk. Neat stacks of paper covered one side of it, a newspaper the other. A fax machine sat in one corner. A computer sat on a desk in another corner, hooked up to a printer. On the walls all around him were huge color photos of Sandy Peterson and the racecar team. On a shelf was a radio, playing the music.

"I really need to make a phone call," I said, "and the nearest pay phone is across the track. May I borrow your phone? I can charge the call to my uncle's calling card."

"I guess so," Tim Becker said.

"Thank you," I said. It hit me that maybe I had imagined a little too much. If I was wrong, I was about to make a dumb phone call. "Um, would it be okay if it was a private call?"

"Sure, why not?" he said. He pushed his chair back and grabbed the newspaper from his desk.

"Just shout when you're finished," he said, letting the screen door bang shut behind him.

I picked up the telephone. I called directory assistance. I got the number for the San Diego Zoo. Uncle Mike had given me his calling card number because I often needed to make calls for him. I used that number, and less than a minute later I was talking to the trainer.

I told him what I was looking for. He told me it was one of the cameramen who had asked about mice, first thing in the morning. I thanked him.

I hung up the phone.

I walked outside. Tim Becker was sitting on the bottom step of the trailer, reading his newspaper.

"Thanks," I said.

He looked up from the sports pages.

"You're welcome," he answered. He folded the newspaper.

He stepped aside to make room for me. I hopped down the stairs and headed back toward Uncle Mike's motor home. My mind was definitely not on where I was going.

One of the cameramen had asked about mice and elephants. Early in the morning. Like early enough to fill the cooler with mice. But why?

Almost at Uncle Mike's motor home, I saw the door to the neighboring motor home open. The one where Brian Nelson and Al Simonsen were staying, two of the cameramen who had worked the San Diego shoot.

Normally, I would have kept walking and shouted hello to whoever was coming out. But not after talking to the elephant trainer.

I ducked behind the side of another trailer and watched as Brian Nelson left his trailer. He was in a hurry.

Was this truly strange, I wondered, or was I working too hard? Was I imagining there was a bad guy in this?

I kept watching as he got farther away from me. A couple of times he looked around, like he was worried about being followed.

Here's one of the funny things about people. When someone drops his voice to a whisper, it's a sure sign that he doesn't want to be heard. And, of course, that's the thing that makes people curious enough to try to listen when before they wouldn't have cared.

I had the same response as soon as I thought Brian didn't want to be followed. Especially after talking to the elephant trainer. It made me want to follow him.

Which I did.

The infield wasn't crowded with people, but there were enough around that I could hang back as Brian picked and pushed his way among them.

He didn't notice me.

His journey was a short one. It took him straight to Tim Becker's trailer, where I had just borrowed the phone.

More strange. From the beginning of this shoot, I'd never seen Brian talking with Tim, not even at the barbecue. They weren't friends. So why would Brian be going there now, when he was supposed to be helping Uncle Mike? And why did Brian look so nervous? What was going on?

I moved to the edge of another motor home, keeping out of sight. I was still half the length of a football field away, with maybe half a dozen other trailers lining the pavement between us. It was close enough, though, to clearly see Tim Becker's face when he answered the knock on his door.

Tim looked angry.

He looked around, then pulled Brian Nelson inside. Quickly. Like he didn't want anyone to see them together.

Enough weird things had happened that I decided I wasn't imagining things. Brian was someplace I hadn't expected him to be. And he'd looked guilty getting there. Tim didn't want him there. Yet Tim had quickly pulled Brian into the trailer anyway.

I made a decision. At the back of Tim's trailer, next to his desk, was a window. While I was on the phone, I had noticed it was open.

I told myself that if they talked loud enough for me to overhear, it wasn't really like spying. And that if they didn't have anything to hide, they wouldn't be mad that I had listened.

So I moved quietly around the side of the trailer and stood beneath the window.

chapter eighteen

"To me, it's simple," I heard Brian Nelson say. "I did my job. The shoot is over. All the film in the can is trashed. I want to get paid."

Film? Trashed? What did he mean, trashed?

"And I told you," Tim Becker said. "Not until Hiser misses the deadline completely. Once I am guaranteed he can't produce the show, you will get paid."

"No chance he's going to make it now," Brian said. "I just told you. Whatever filming was done is useless. I want my money so

I can quit and get out of here before they can blame me."

"Tomorrow," Tim said. "But don't come here to get it. Call me. Last thing I want is for someone to see us together."

"Not tomorrow," Brian Nelson said. "This afternoon. And I want an extra five thousand dollars."

"You're nuts. You're already getting ten thousand."

"Look," Brian said. "I'm not stupid. I watched you all through that barbecue. You brought us our fruit salads. It wasn't until I heard what the doctor said that I realized what you had done. You could have at least warned me."

"And if you were the only one not sick," Tim said, "it would have looked strange."

"Fair enough," Brian said. "But it's worth an extra five grand. Or maybe you'd like me to go back to the same reporter you sent me to with the other story."

"Fine, fine," Tim Becker said. "I'll have the money for you this afternoon."

"Cash," Brian Nelson insisted.

"Are you absolutely sure the film is use-less?"

"I know my business."

"All right then," Tim agreed. "Cash."

Brian Nelson? Getting money from Tim Becker? Getting money to mess up Uncle Mike's deadline?

I didn't understand. I wondered what to do next.

I heard the screen door open and close. I pushed back farther into the shadows. I wondered if I should follow Brian.

Before I could decide, I heard a tiny bip, bip, bip. It came through the open window. I was so close to Tim Becker that I could actually hear him punching in numbers on his telephone.

Bip, bip, bip. There was a pause. Then I clearly heard Tim speak. "Hello, Linda. Can you put me through? It's Tim."

Another pause. I guessed Tim was waiting to be put through.

"Yeah," Tim said. "Just want you to know that the production crew is on the way out. They don't have any useable footage. There's no way Hiser can turn out an hour of prime time. You shouldn't have any problem squeezing him now."

Squeezing him?

There was another pause as I tried to figure that out.

"Okay," Tim said. "Just remember, I get to L.A. next week. You keep all that money warm and waiting for me."

There was silence as he listened. Then he laughed. "Yes, get me an office with a view. I'm looking forward to my new job."

He hung up.

My mind went into instant knots. I had just heard a very valuable clue to figuring out why so many things had gone wrong with the shoot. But who had Tim Becker called? And how could I find out?

Well, I answered myself, I could just march in there and ask him. And, of course, he would just tell me. Right.

Hang on, I thought. Maybe his telephone could tell me.

But I needed to get in there right away.

I walked quickly back to the door. I knocked loudly.

Tim came to the door and seemed surprised to see me again. "What's up?" he asked pleasantly. Like he was actually a nice guy.

That was a good question. One I wanted to ask him right back. The two-faced snake.

Then I realized he was staring at me. He expected an answer to his question about what was up. And why I had come back to his trailer.

"Well...," I said. All right, I thought, if you're lying to me, I'll get you back by telling the truth. "Well...I need to borrow your phone again."

He gave me a crooked grin. "A person might think you had a girlfriend."

Again, he grabbed the newspaper from his desk.

"I know, I know," he said as he walked out the door. "Private call. I'll leave you alone."

"That would be great," I said. Very, very great. "I won't be long."

He let the door bang behind him.

I picked up the telephone, hoping I had guessed right.

I saw the Redial button.

I grinned. A real grin, not the kind that Tim Becker used on people.

I hit Redial.

I heard the tones of the numbers dialing at high speed. Bip, bip, bip, bip, bip, bip, bip, bip, bip, bip, bip.

So far, so good. I held my breath as I waited for the phone to connect.

It began to ring.

Even better than good. Would I find out who was on the other end?

"Globewide Studios," a woman said in a pleasant voice. "John Greeley's office."

I was so stunned I did exactly nothing. Globewide Studios? John Greeley? As in John Greeley, president of one of the world's largest entertainment companies? As in the John Greeley who was negotiating for Uncle Mike's script?

"Hello?" the woman's voice said. "Hello?"

I hung up the phone.

chapter nineteen

Uncle Mike had finished his phone calls. I found him back inside the motor home.

He sat on the edge of a chair. His elbows were on his knees. His face in his hands. Not a picture of happiness.

"What happened?" I asked. "Did someone make you watch an hour of *Barney*?"

"Worse," Uncle Mike said. "I called someone at Lone Coyote to ask for an extension on the documentary deadline and he just laughed. Then I tried to call Globewide

Studios. Remember, the people who were so hot to buy the Viola Moses script? But all I got was a runaround. The president, John Greeley, used to talk to me any time. Now, his secretary won't put me through, and I'm not even sure John is getting my messages. At this moment, things don't look good."

I wasn't sure this was the time to tell him exactly how bad everything looked.

"You can sell the option to someone else, can't you?" I asked. "If that script was worth so much to Globewide..."

"Timing," he said with a heavy sigh, "is everything."

"Meaning?"

"It will take less than a day for word to get out about how badly this shoot has gone. And it will look like I don't have any control over my crew when people read that newspaper report. You think anyone will hire me as a director of a major film when I can't even pull a simple one-hour documentary together? As for the option, yeah, maybe I'll find a buyer. But again, it's all about timing."

He got up and started pacing. "If Sandy fires us, I'll have to pay Lone Coyote the penalty for not delivering the documentary. If I miss that payment, they can file proceedings against me to force me into bankruptcy. That means I'll have to unload the option fast. That means everyone will know I'm desperate to sell. And that means I'll have to take a lower price. That's why I wanted to reach John Greeley to make a deal. Today. Before he discovers how much trouble I'm in."

"Um," I said. I didn't want to do it, but sooner or later I'd have to tell Uncle Mike what I knew. "I was over at Tim Becker's trailer and—"

His cell phone rang and interrupted me.

"Hiser here," he said as he answered.

His face lit up with a smile. "John Greeley! I'm glad you got my message. Thanks for calling back."

Uncle Mike stopped pacing. He gave me a thumbs-up.

"Yes," Uncle Mike said into the telephone. "I've been thinking about your offer on the Viola Moses script. I just want you to know that I'd be interested in closing the deal on the amount we discussed."

Seconds later, he frowned. "I see. Yes, thank you. Good-bye."

He snapped his cell phone shut. For a moment he just stood there, saying nothing. He looked like a fish gasping for air.

"He's changed his mind," Uncle Mike said. "Globewide doesn't want anything to do with my script. My best buyer is no longer willing to give me even a dollar for it. How can that be?"

"Um," I said again. "I was over at Tim Becker's trailer and—"

Again, his ringing cell phone interrupted me.

"Hiser here," Uncle Mike said. This time, no smile as he listened.

"A deal?" Uncle Mike said. "What kind of deal?"

He listened more. His face got darker and darker. Like the face of a fish about to stop gasping for air.

Finally, Uncle Mike spoke. "I'll think about it."

That was the end of the conversation.

"I can't believe it," he said. "That was someone from Lone Coyote. He offered to buy my production company. For the million dollars I will owe them if I miss my deadline. It's almost like he knew that Globewide had just said no."

"I think he did," I said quietly.

Finally, I told Uncle Mike everything I had overheard at Tim Becker's trailer.

His jaw dropped as he listened.

"In other words," he said when I finished, "Globewide and Lone Coyote were both working against me?"

"That's my guess," I said. "Lone Coyote suckered you with a contract they made sure you couldn't handle. Who knows? Maybe Globewide will come back with some super-low offer for the Viola Moses script, and Lone Coyote will get the chance to work with Globewide on it. And from what I heard, it sounds like Tim Becker has just gotten himself a great new job in Hollywood."

"No," Uncle Mike said. "Somehow, we're going to use what we have and patch it together. Once Sandy Peterson knows about Tim Becker, I believe she'll give us the chance to finish."

I shook my head no. I had saved the worst for last.

"I think that all the filmwork is gone," I said. "Brian Nelson said he'd trashed it. He was trying to collect his money so he could get out of here."

"What?!"

Uncle Mike left me behind as he ran out of the motor home.

I followed.

In the other motor home, we discovered Brian Nelson had spoken the truth to Tim Becker.

Someone had poured vinegar on all the film and video footage.

There was no chance of rescuing it. Or of rescuing the documentary.

chapter twenty

"This is the end of life as I know it," Uncle Mike groaned. "I might as well buy a broom and learn to sweep. That's the only work I'll be able to get in Hollywood."

Me too, I thought. Where else was I going to be able to get the inside track? No more summers with Uncle Mike. No chance of working with him on a feature film. Was life even worth living?

I got more depressed.

But Uncle Mike got angry.

"Come on," he said. "Tim Becker is going to pay. We're going to hear the truth from him. And we're going to use that."

I was so depressed I didn't even care about revenge.

"What good will that do?" I said. "We can't prove any of this. Not in court. Probably not even to Sandy Peterson."

"You overheard Tim Becker talking to Brian Nelson and to Globewide," Uncle Mike said.

"I did," I said. "But it would be my word against his. I'm only seventeen. He's a professional public relations man. Who's going to believe me over him?"

Uncle Mike slammed his right fist into his left palm. "There's got to be some way. I mean, you heard him admit that he poisoned a bunch of us."

Poisoned a bunch of us. I knew that too well, because I'd been there. I remembered the feeling vividly.

Then it hit me. I'd been there. And I'd had my handheld camera.

"Uncle Mike," I said, "there's a slight, slight chance we might have something."

"What's that?" he asked.

I explained.

It took us two hours. We spent the first hour going through my film at high speed, just to find the sections that I had filmed during the barbecue. Then we ran the barbecue portion at normal speed.

Because I had spent so much time with the camera on my shoulder, by then everyone had even forgotten I was filming.

I had caught the crew laughing. I had caught some people stuffing their faces with watermelon, the juice dribbling down their chins. I had caught bits and pieces of racing conversations. And, buried deep in that footage, there was a shot of Tim Becker in the background, just after everyone had eaten the main course.

The footage was dark and a little shaky. We had to slow it down and use the computer to enhance the image. But we saw it. I had footage of Tim Becker pouring berries from a small plastic bag into a serving of fruit salad.

"Got him!" Uncle Mike crowed. He slapped me on the back. "Man, oh man. You were a filming machine. You've got everything that's happened in the last few weeks. I can't wait to show our evidence to Sandy Peterson!"

chapter twenty-one

Twenty minutes later, I was back in Tim Becker's trailer. But I wasn't by myself this time. Uncle Mike stood on one side of me. Sandy Peterson stood on the other. I had my camera on my shoulder, ready to record what would happen next.

"What's going on?" Tim asked. He waved at my camera. He started to rise from his chair. "A new segment for the documentary?"

"Don't bother getting up," Sandy told him.

"Huh?"

Her tone was angry. He, of course, didn't know why. He was about to, though.

"I've been confused and bothered by all the little things that have made it tough for the racing team lately," Sandy said. "I'm not confused anymore."

I swung my camera from her to Tim to catch his reply.

"I don't understand," he said. My camera caught every expression on his face.

"Oh, but I do," she said. "Nice little scam you had going. You paid Brian Nelson to mess things up for the film crew. And since you have a pass to go wherever you want in the pit, you found ways to mess up my team too. You might have gotten me killed, messing with my car. Just so the film crew misses the deadline, and you get a great new job with Globewide Studios."

"What are you talking about?" he said. "None of that is true."

"Don't even think you can fool me," she said. "Trenton and Mike might not know John Greeley is your uncle, but I do. You used him as a reference when you applied for this job. Remember? You said it wouldn't hurt for my racing team to have a connection right to the top in Hollywood."

"You can't prove anything," Tim Becker said. He looked straight into my camera. "She is telling lies. If she tries to accuse me publicly, I will sue her for it."

"I've got something on video that proves at least part of it," she said. She placed the plastic cassette on his desk. "Trenton here filmed you putting the poisonous elderberries in the fruit salad. I think that's a good start. And you can bet we'll work hard to prove the rest of it."

Tim picked up the cassette and turned it over a few times in his hands. He did not seem too upset.

He stood up, keeping the cassette in his hands.

I saw him through my viewfinder as he walked closer to me.

"I feel confident about my original statement," he said casually, as if we were discussing the weather.

He tucked the cassette under his belt as he walked closer, still talking. "You can't prove anything."

In a quick movement, he filled my viewfinder completely. Before I could figure out what had happened, he had grabbed me by the shoulders. He pulled a ballpoint pen from his pocket and stuck the sharp end of it against my throat.

It hurt. Bad. I wondered if I was bleeding. If he pushed any harder, the pen could bust through my windpipe.

He continued, still sounding oddly casual, "Like I said. When I take this kid's camera and walk out of here with the videocassette, there is definitely nothing you can prove. Like you can't prove I poisoned the film crew and lied about being sick myself when the doctor called. Like you can't prove that I paid Brian Nelson to create problems as often as possible. And he did a good job too. Messing up the elephant shoot with mice was a stroke of genius. And making sure your camera equipment ended up in the wrong place was exactly the kind of thing I'd have done in his place..."

I gasped at the pain as he pushed the pen harder against my neck.

"Don't hurt him," Uncle Mike said. "It's not worth it. To you or to us."

"Then don't make a move toward me," Tim answered. He was breathing heavily. This close to him, I could feel the fabric of his shirt against my cheek. I smelled after-shave and a trace of sweat.

"We won't do anything," Sandy said. "Let the kid go."

"Back up," Tim said. "Get behind my desk."

Neither of them moved.

Tim jabbed the pen deeper in my neck. I gasped again.

The others quickly walked around the desk.

"Stay there," he told them.

"Why?" Sandy said. "Why would you do this?"

"Get a life," Tim said. "Anyone would do it for what I'm getting paid—and for the new job I'll start next week."

"No," Uncle Mike said. "What you're doing is wrong."

Tim kept the pen pressed against my windpipe.

"Don't make me laugh," he said. "I've been watching you and your nephew. You don't let anything get in the way of your ambition either."

"We don't try to destroy another's livelihood for our own gain, and we don't threaten kids," Uncle Mike said.

"But you wrecked your marriage," Tim said. "I heard all about that from the camera crew. How you ignored your wife and kids so long that they became strangers. And Trenton here, he's a kid, but he's got no life. He's going to end up just like you."

"He focuses totally, with that camera glued to his body. He has no life but filming. I've listened to him talk about what he wants to do. I haven't heard him once say anything about his family. Neither of you has time for anything or anyone beyond your ambitions. Don't call me selfish when the only difference between you and me is that I don't try to fool myself about my ambition."

He jerked me toward the door.

"Sandy, Mike, get down on your stomachs behind the desk."

They did. I was glad. I didn't want the pen stuck any deeper than it was.

Tim opened the door with his free hand. He made some movements with his fingers that I could not see, only hear.

He laughed in my ear. "Hey, I work for my uncle. You work for yours. And we're both using family connections to get ahead."

Without warning, he kicked my feet out from under me. I hit the floor.

He grabbed the camera as I was falling. He ran out, slamming the door behind him.

I began to get up as Uncle Mike and Sandy ran toward me, and we bumped into one another.

"He's getting away!" Uncle Mike shouted. He pushed me out of the way and grabbed for the door.

It wouldn't open.

That's what Tim had been doing. Locking the door.

It took another few seconds of rattling the handle for Uncle Mike to unlock the door.

By the time we got outside, there was no sign of Tim Becker. Or of my handheld camera. Or of the cassette with the film that could prove what he had been doing.

chapter twenty-two

"There's only one way he can get out of here," Sandy said. "And that's by car. Let's head to the parking lot."

All of us began to run. We ignored the strange looks from people walking the paths between the motor homes.

"What if he dumps the video and camera somewhere?" Uncle Mike asked, half yelling.

"He'll be too afraid someone might find it," she said. "He'll keep it with him until he's far from here."

I saw movement out of the corner of my eye. To the right, I saw someone sprawled on the ground. I also heard angry shouts.

"That way!" I pointed. I saw Tim's back as he ducked behind another motor home. "He's over there."

Uncle Mike and Sandy stopped.

"But the parking lot is to our left," she said.

"I know," I said. "But that's not the only place to get a car."

"Pit road!" Uncle Mike and Sandy said at the same time.

We ran toward the track.

"I don't get it," Uncle Mike said. "He's going to run in circles?"

"If he can get to the far end," Sandy said, "he can cut down through the infield and out that way."

She wasn't even breathing hard. It showed me how drivers had to be in good shape to compete.

"And if he can get away from the track," she said over her shoulder as we worked hard to keep up, "and dump the video some place we can't find, it will be worth whatever he gets fined for taking a stock car on the streets. We've got to stop him!"

We got there just as Tim reached an empty idling car pitted in the middle row. Because all the crew recognized him, they weren't concerned when he wandered up to the car. Without warning, he dove into the front seat and scrambled to get behind the steering wheel. The crew was too far away to do anything as Tim roared away with squealing tires.

"What now?" I shouted.

Sandy didn't answer. She was already halfway to another crew.

"Give me your car," she yelled to them as she approached. "I've got to stop him!"

People jumped out of her way.

Seconds later, she was in hot pursuit.

I saw it later on a television news show. A fan in the stands had been filming the cars as drivers did some test runs. There had been only one car on the track.

When the second car—with Tim Becker driving—burst onto the track, it became interesting. And the fan filmed both cars.

Sandy Peterson's car really made it confusing.

The first driver, thinking he had the whole track to himself, almost hit Tim as he roared out of pit road.

Sandy, a better driver and able to get through her gears faster, almost hit them both as she came out on Tim's tail.

The first driver spun out and trailed smoke and dust all the way to the bottom of the track.

Sandy stayed on Tim's bumper.

They screamed through the first turn.

Through the second turn. Tim still had the lead.

One more turn and Tim would be able to hit the track low and escape through the infield.

Unless Sandy found a way to stop him.

She started the third turn high, with Tim taking the middle.

She swept down and cut beneath him.

Instead of passing, she stayed right at his side, taking away the bottom of the track.

Then she pressed her car against his.

Metal shrieked against metal.

He swung his wheel. But she was expecting it and turned her car harder into his. Sparks flew like fireworks from the bodies of both cars.

The screaming of metal against metal grew louder and louder as the cars slowed.

She pushed him higher up on the track. Higher. Higher. Until the other side of his car began to grind against the concrete wall.

By this time, they had slowed to under thirty miles an hour.

She ground him into the wall until both cars had stopped. She wedged her car against his and jumped out.

Angrily, she walked up to his window.

And she punched him in the nose.

The crowd went crazy.

But even with Tim Becker trapped, Uncle Mike still faced the worst part of all.

Without any footage and with the deadline coming up, he was still about to lose his company. And a script that might be worth an Oscar.

chapter twenty-three

That afternoon, when everything had settled down, I found a pay phone near a concession stand. I dialed a number. I didn't use Uncle Mike's calling card. This wasn't business. I called collect.

"Mom?" I said after she agreed to pay for the call and the operator had hung up. "It's Trent."

Not Trenton. Suddenly that seemed too much, like I was trying to make myself sound too important.

"Trent!" Her voice was as surprised as it was happy.

I could picture her wide smile and short ash-blond hair. It broke my heart that she sounded so happy and surprised. I should have been calling a lot, so that this call wasn't a surprise.

"Trent!" she said again. But now her voice sounded worried. "Are you all right?"

That broke my heart too, that she thought the only reason I would call was if something was wrong.

"I'm all right," I said. "I just miss you guys."

That was true. I'd had some time to think about what Tim Becker had said. I'd been wrong to think only about my dreams. There was much more to life than work.

"We miss you," she said. "Your dad and I pray for you every day when you're so far away."

"He's doing good?" I asked.

"Yes, he's doing well."

We both laughed. Mom's an English teacher.

"How's the weather?" she asked.

"Good," I said. Maybe some people would have found it boring to listen to us. Right at that moment, though, I realized it wasn't what we were saying that was important. It was how we were saying it, and why. We were family, and the words were just an excuse for us to let the other know it was important to be connected.

"Is Jody's beach volleyball team winning?" I asked. My sister was a great player. I decided I would take time to go to her games when I got back.

"They have a shot at the championship," Mom said. "How's the shoot going with Uncle Mike?"

"I'll tell you all about it when we get back," I said. I didn't want to worry her. "I think we'll be home soon."

"Great," she said.

We talked a while longer. She didn't ask why I had called out of the blue. She didn't make me feel bad for taking so long to call.

And at the end of the call, she said something that I'd heard a lot of other times.

But today it meant more to me than it had in the past.

"Take care," she said. "We love you."

I smiled at the blank wall of the phone booth.

"I love you guys too."

An hour later, I met Sandy and Uncle Mike in his motor home.

"We've talked to some lawyers," Uncle Mike said. "Things don't look good."

Sandy shook her head, her lips tight and grim. "Not good at all. They're saying it will be next to impossible to prove anything, not if Brian Nelson and Tim Becker both decide to keep lying about things. We might not even be able to prove Tim put the elderberries in the fruit salad; the video shot isn't clear enough. As it is now, all they can do is charge Tim with reckless driving or auto theft. Which is nothing compared to proving the rest of it."

"Oh," I said. "I'm sorry to hear that. I guess we won't be able to get an extension on the documentary. I know you were hoping it would help you with your sponsor."

"Hang on," Uncle Mike said quickly. "Don't think we're giving up. Both Sandy and I would really like to find a way to punish the studios for what they've done."

They exchanged smiles. Obviously they had talked about this already.

"Yeah," Sandy said. "It will probably hurt Lone Coyote if they have to pay your Uncle Mike the million-dollar bonus they agreed to in the contract."

"I'm not sure I understand," I said.

"Well," Uncle Mike answered, "I doubt they ever planned on having to pay that much money. All along, they thought Tim Becker would find a way to stop us. If they suddenly have to cough up a million dollars..."

"Tim Becker did stop us," I said. "He slowed production to a standstill. He made Sandy and her crew look bad. And he ruined all the film we shot. You don't have anything to make the documentary with—and there's not time to get more film pulled together before the deadline."

Uncle Mike grinned. "He didn't ruin all the film."

"I was there," I said. "I saw it. Brian Nelson wrecked it all."

"I repeat," Uncle Mike said, "not all of it."

Sandy broke in. "Your Uncle Mike says if I can finish well tomorrow, that's all the footage he'll need to make the documentary one of the most exciting one-hour spots anyone has seen for our sport. He says he can go into post-production next week with everything he has and be finished by the deadline. All he needs is my approval, and Lone Coyote will have to pay one million dollars. And trust me, the documentary will get my approval."

"I still don't get it," I said. I really didn't. And I couldn't figure out why Uncle Mike stood there grinning at me like I had just won a cutest baby contest.

"Trent," he said, "Brian Nelson didn't break into our motor home."

"Huh? I mean, pardon me?"

"Let me tell you," Uncle Mike said. "You have a great eye and a lot of natural talent. I've been going over your footage a lot more slowly. You've captured some great stuff, and from some great angles."

"Are you saying...?" I could hardly believe him.

"Yes," he said. "We can easily pull an hour's worth of stuff from the footage you've shot. It will have a music video feel to it that is really hip. I'm telling you, you are good. And if we can cap it with a strong finish, we'll have an award-winning documentary. With your name all over it."

"Wow," I said, hardly able to breathe. "Wow."

I looked over at Sandy.

"Please," I said. "Please run hard tomorrow."

chapter twenty-four

Before the race began, I wanted to ask George Lot about the strategy he intended to use.

"Would you mind if I asked you a question and filmed your answer?" I asked him. Before I would have just done it, thinking that the most important thing in the world was me and my job. Now I knew better.

"Fire away," he said. He was a lot friendlier now, knowing that Tim Becker had been behind all the trouble.

Sigmund Brouwer

"How's she going to win this one?"
I asked. "What's the plan?"

It seemed that the pit road beyond us
was getting more and more crowded as cars
zoomed in and out during their final adjustments. I leaned in closer to hear him above
the noise.

"This is a four-hundred-lap race, and we're
going to try to make it with as few pit stops
as possible. This track is tricky. It's short
and there's little room for mistakes. And
that shows up in the number of yellow flags
this track averages. Over the last five years,
each race has seen at least five yellow flags.
We're going to stretch our stops as far apart
as possible."

"That sounds like regular public relations
stuff to me," I said. I adjusted my focus to
catch every twitch on his face. "We need the
inside scoop."

His smile looked good on a face that was
usually set in stone.

"Here's what we'd never let any of the
other teams know before a race," he said.
"Her slow qualifying run hurt. She's starting

so far back that we're going to have to keep her out there until she's running on vapors. If she can get in even two more laps on everyone else before she comes in to the pits, yellow flags will really help us."

"That sounds risky," I said. "What if she runs out of fuel?"

"Don't ask," George Lot said. "Don't even ask."

I stayed in the pit area behind the wall as all the cars went through their pace lap. As always, I filmed everything I could.

It felt great, knowing that Uncle Mike believed in me. I could hardly wait to tell Mom and Dad about this weekend.

There was a radio scanner nearby, and it let me hear the pre-race instructions to the pace car driver: "Give us sixty-five all around the track."

Sixty-five miles per hour. The pace car would keep everybody at that speed as all the cars settled into their positions. Sandy would be starting at thirty-first.

I heard the instructions to all the pit crew chiefs: "Crew chiefs, remind your drivers not to pass anyone until they reach the start/finish line."

George Lot, standing down the wall from me, spoke into his radio, relaying the message to Sandy.

Seconds later, the pace car entered pit road. And seconds after that, the race began with all engines howling.

It was the first turn that drivers had to worry about. There, as they fought for position, the pack would be bunched so tight that there could easily be a wreck or two.

I had my camera on my shoulder, ready to move and film anything that happened in the pit. But I took a moment to look up at the monitor first. Sandy stayed well back as the pack moved into the turn. If there was going to be a wreck, she wouldn't be part of it. And if it knocked five or seven cars out of the race, it would move her up all those positions.

No wreck. She kept her position. And all of the cars shot into the straightaway.

I settled back into trying to shoot what I could in the pit.

I got some close-ups of the pit crew in their fire suits, staring at the track.

I took an upward angle of George Lot. He frowned at me. Which was good. It made him look even more serious and concerned.

I got some still shots of the organized tires, tools and fuel, ready for the pit stops.

And around me, I heard the chatter.

"She's moved up four spots."

"Eight laps to pit."

"Tire temperature holding."

Four laps later, there was a yellow flag. One of the middle cars blew an engine, and it took two laps of yellow before the track was cleared.

That gave Sandy time to come in for her first pit.

I watched through my camera as I filmed her up close.

"You're doing good," George told her. "Lots of cars pitted earlier during green. Keep your concentration going."

Sweat poured off her face. In my camera, the drops of moisture were shiny beads.

Excellent, I told myself, great footage.

Twenty seconds later, she was gone.

Another twenty seconds later, three more cars were gone. Not from pit road like Sandy. But gone from the race.

The second-place car had bumped the leader as it passed, and both of them slid sideways together. The body metal of both cars shrieked at the high-speed stress.

A third car hit them both, and in a spinning whirl that threw debris in all directions, the pile slid down the track toward the infield.

Immediate yellow.

Fire trucks raced toward them and covered the cars in a sea of white foam.

On the track, Sandy called to George on the radio.

"I'm coming back in. Those cars bled some oil and I think the track's going to be slick. Let's adjust the wedge while we can."

I swung my camera to George.

"Get ready," he barked to the crew.

Sandy roared into the pit.

I ran down the wall to get a better view with my camera. I knew what she meant by wedge. We could add a voice-over on the segment I was about to film so viewers would understand the term too.

The voice-over would explain that since the racecar drivers go only one direction around the track, it helps if the car is tilted back slightly. Like a table with shorter legs on the front right and left rear corners. If you wad a piece of paper and stick it under the front right leg, the table will tilt back onto the shorter left rear corner. And vice versa.

The wedge on the car did the same thing, only on the front right and left rear tires. By tilting the car back just slightly, it could hang through the corners better or worse, depending on the adjustment.

Again, it took less than thirty seconds for her to get in and out.

I heard the scanner: Debris had been cleared from the track. The drivers were back to a green flag.

Over the next two hours, Sandy moved up steadily until, in the final five laps, she was in second place.

Second place!

People in the pit were on their feet, cheering and shouting. Except for George.

I snuck up behind him. I wanted to contrast their excitement against his calmness. His shoulders and head and neck filled my viewfinder. Just beyond him, out of focus, were crew members in their red coveralls.

I knew my job was just to stay out of the way. Especially in the heat of the race. But it looked like I could slip in for a second.

"George," I said. "Is she going to win?"

George turned and faced the camera squarely.

"She's got three laps to go and maybe only two and half laps of fuel. But if we had pitted her at any time, she would have lost a lap to the leader. If she can find a way to save fuel, she's got a chance. But if she throttles back to save fuel, she won't hold her position. Now leave me alone."

It got so exciting that I nearly set my camera down to watch the last few laps. And in the last minutes of a race that had taken three hours, I understood why victory was so precious. Defeat and heartbreak were always a heartbeat away, no matter how close a driver was to victory.

In the second to last turn, the leader blew a tire. Later, I would find out that he and his pit chief had gambled too, trying to stretch out tires and fuel between stops.

The blown tire sent him into the wall and out of the race.

Leaving Sandy in first place.

Until she ran out of fuel.

George had called it exactly.

She ran out in the final turn.

It was agony to watch her coast toward the finish, but losing speed. With two other cars catching up fast.

I found myself shouting along with the pit crew.

"Go! Go! Go!"

If voices could propel a car, she would have gained speed. Everyone in the pit was shouting that loud.

The other two cars began to catch her.

Closer, closer, closer.

And then they passed her.

So why was everyone around me cheering?

Then I figured it out. I'd been so worried about the cars behind her, I hadn't seen that she was moving closer, closer to the finish line. And that she had coasted to first place, half a car ahead of the other two.

She'd won!

I ran over to George Lot and gave him my handheld camera. I asked him to point it at me.

I stepped back.

I raised my arms in the air and grinned at the camera.

I wanted this on film. Not for the documentary. But for my family.

Because it was about time I shared my life with them. And this was a good place to start.

Sigmund Brouwer is the best-selling author of many books for children and young adults. He has contributed to the Orca Currents series (*Wired, Sewer Rats*) and the Orca Sports series (most recently *Winter Hawk Star, Hurricane Power* and *Hitmen Triumph*). He and his family live in Red Deer, Alberta, and Eagleville, Tennessee.

orca sports

All-Star Pride
Sigmund Brouwer

Blazer Drive
Sigmund Brouwer

Chief Honor
Sigmund Brouwer

Cobra Strike
Sigmund Brouwer

Crossover
Jeff Rud

Dead in the Water
Robin Stevenson

Hitmen Triumph
Sigmund Brouwer

Hurricane Power
Sigmund Brouwer

Jumper
Michele Martin Bossley

Kicker
Michele Martin Bossley

Rebel Glory
Sigmund Brouwer

Scarlet Thunder
Sigmund Brouwer

Tiger Threat
Sigmund Brouwer

Titan Clash
Sigmund Brouwer

Two Foot Punch
Anita Daher

Winter Hawk Star
Sigmund Brouwer

Visit www.orcabook.com for more Orca titles.